DISCLAIMER

The author and publisher are providing this book and its contents on an "as is" basis and make no representations or warranties of any kind with respect to this book or its contents. The author and publisher disclaim all such representations and warranties, including but not limited to warranties of merchantability. In addition, the author and publisher do not represent or warrant that the information accessible via this book is accurate, complete, or current.

Except as specifically stated in this book, neither the author nor publisher, nor any authors, contributors, or other representatives will be liable for damages arising out of or in connection with the use of this book. This is a comprehensive limitation of liability that applies to all damages of any kind, including (without limitation) compensatory; direct, indirect, or consequential damages; loss of data, income, or profit; loss of or damage to property; and claims of third parties.

FIRST EDITION - Published 2022

Extra Graphic Material From: www.freepik.com
Thanks to: Alekksall, Starline, Pch.vector, Rawpixel.com, Vectorpocket, Dgim-studio, Upklyak, Macrovector, Stockgiu, Pikisuperstar & Freepik.com Designers

This Book Comes With Free Bonus Puzzles

Available Here:

BestActivityBooks.com/WSBONUS20

5 TIPS TO START!

1) HOW TO SOLVE

The Puzzles are in a Classic Format:

- Words are hidden without breaks (no spaces, dashes, ...)
- Orientation: Forward & Backward, Up & Down or
  in Diagonal (can be in both directions)
- Words can overlap or cross each other

2) ACTIVE LEARNING

To encourage learning actively, a space is provided next to each word to write down the translation. The **DICTIONARY** allows you to verify and expand your knowledge. You can look up and write down each translation, find the words in the Puzzle then add them to your vocabulary!

3) TAG YOUR WORDS

Have you tried using a tag system? For example, you could mark the words which have been difficult to find with a cross, the ones you loved with a star, new words with a triangle, rare words with a diamond and so on...

4) ORGANIZE YOUR LEARNING

We also offer a convenient **NOTEBOOK** at the end of this edition. Whether on vacation, travelling or at home, you can easily organize your new knowledge without needing a second notebook!

5) FINISHED?

Go to the bonus section: **MONSTER CHALLENGE** to find a free game offered at the end of this edition!

Want more fun and learning activities? It's **Fast and Simple!**
An entire Game Book Collection just **one click away!**

Find your next challenge at:

BestActivityBooks.com/MyNextWordSearch

Ready, Set... Go!

Did you know there are around 7,000 different languages in the world? Words are precious.

We love languages and have been working hard to make the highest quality books for you. Our ingredients?

A selection of indispensable learning themes, three big slices of fun, then we add a spoonful of difficult words and a pinch of rare ones. We serve them up with care and a maximum of delight so you can solve the best word games and have fun learning!

Your feedback is essential. You can be an active participant in the success of this book by leaving us a review. Tell us what you liked most in this edition!

Here is a short link which will take you to your order page.

BestBooksActivity.com/Review50

Thanks for your help and enjoy the Game!

Linguas Classics Team

1 - Antiques

```
P R A R T I K O S Y R A S Z
Y O R A M O T A J N O A T A
F A N A K A E I V A O Q I V
I Y A N J A X J H B M G L A
O T F I U F C K A H O L A T
F Q K R S I Z I Y V A E E R
G O O A B P R I C E A K D A
F P M M N Y V M A H X T K Z
A J A B Y T N A V A L N R N
G M P Q A B O A T I L A K A
T S Y M A H A Z A T R A G X
W G H A I N G O N T R A N O
F I R A V A K A R T E H U X
G A L L E R Y J U P V Y J T
```

LAVANTY	ZAVATRA
MARINA	FIRAVAKA
TAONJATO MARO	TALOHA
HETRA	PRICE
TOE-JAVATRA	KALITAO
HAINGON-TRANO	SARY SOKITRA
KANTO	FOMBA
FANAKA	TSY MAHAZATRA
GALLERY	

2 - Food #1

```
B I E W B S T A P R I C O T
L A G J Y A O R P O A R A Q
H L S Y Y L N A T O E C J Y
P G P I B A G N J H G Z G O
X Y M Y L D O I G K O L K X
K M H C C Y L P U X N N A T
V A K P A D O E U X O E R O
O M N S K O G Z Z J N A A N
A A Y E E W A F Z S O J O G
N R Z K L L S P I N R U T O
J I S D L I Y E L R A B Y L
O S I Z U C N C F R E Z Y O
V A R R L T Q A L A S O P Y
Z V A W R U V T T O F U O S
```

APRICOT	POARA
BARLEY	SALADY
BASIL	SIRA
CAKE	LASOPY
KARAOTY	EPINARA
KANELINA	FREZY
TONGOLO GASY	SIRAMAMY
RONONO	TOFU
TONGOLO	THON
VOANJO	TURNIP

3 - Measurements

```
S E H A T C L A M I C E D M
P H P D H Q A M I P M Y Z I
Q K A E P E L A U T Q W C R
F Y L L S P I R I B P C J E
M W N S U I N G A C G X X F
K C L A R T A T I L U F O Y
H A H A V O N Y K I L A O N
L A M E S A T I A Z G N C P
L A N J A X L A Q G T D B I
B Y T E R A S A O H I S O N
G T Q I H Y S G H N S L K T
G R A M H A R T I N I M Y G
K I L O M E T A T R A N A R
C E N T I M E T E R J Y A X
```

BYTE	HALAVANY
CENTIMETER	LITATRA
DECIMAL	LAMESA
LALINA	MINITRA
GRAM	GRAMA
HAHAVONY	PINT
MIREFY	TAONINA
KILAO	BOKY
KILOMETATRA	LANJA

4 - Farm #2

```
H V I O A J C N Y B B P X H
M P A M B O L Y F P A T G Z
V Y D M G A Z R B O R D D A
T U U V H Q A I I N I I N
T Y V L P W O V J L B T S A
B P O N O N O R T F B C A K
A K A S A M E A D O W T K O
U S N G A N A L I G Q O A N
V V K S Z A O L E H F R F D
I Q A K A S T A K G W N O R
J M Z D S H K Z A B I M S Y
H J O X G L A M A L L O U E
O N D R Y W B M H V W H M F
B A R L E Y G I S A Z T F A
```

BIBY
BARLEY
BARN
KATSAKA
GANA
MPAMBOLY
SAKAFO
VOANKAZO
GISA
ZANAK'ONDRY

LLAMA
MEADOW
RONONO
SAHAM
MASAKA
ONDRY
TCTOR
LEGIOMA
VARY

5 - Books

```
F L Y L A J I N S P R Y Z M
M J J H R D J D M G E W U P
A W E G T O V G U B X Q R A
X K P C E D D E R A X U L M
Y G E Q O S A P N Z L I X A
Z F B P T N I B O T E I O K
A R A T A N T A R A U P T Y
V M A N O D I D I N A R I Y
I T R M A M O R O N A P E C
Z E A R T A R O S I A H M P
A N T M P A N O R A T R A R
V Y N C A S I T R I K A R Y
F K A T O N O N K A L O C C
C L T M P I T A N T A R A I
```

ADVENTURE	MAMORONA
MPANORATRA	HAISORATRA
TOETRA	MPITANTARA
MANODIDINA	TANTARA
DUALITY	PEJY
EPIC	TONONKALO
ARA-TANTARA	MPAMAKY
VAZIVAZY	NIJALY
ASITRIKA	TENY

6 - Meditation

```
F Z I N N T Y A M F H F F F
F A A J P F R A I I U I A A
I N N J S A E K A A L H N H
H A I G N T J I I D Y E D A
E R A L O A I S N A M T I S
T A S O G R F T A N O S N A
S Z T Y F T A E I A Z E I M
I A A P M E B H P N I H H B
K H R A Q O M F A A K A A A
A A A V L T O F T N A M N R
N F U A L A F D F O A P A A
I A A Z A H O F I M N O N N
A J Q A N E K E N A F Y N A
S G R M Z O J D Z L E E G D
```

NY FANEKENA   ARA-TSAINA
MIFOHAZA   SAINA
MIAINA   HETSIKA
TONY   MOZIKA
MAZAVA   TOETRA
FANGORAHANA   FANDINIHANA
FIHETSEHAM-PO   FIADANANA
FAHAZARANA   FOMBA FIJERY
FAHASAMBARANA   FIHETSIKA

7 - Days and Months

```
V J Z T Y D F A O G Z R A D
U O S R N B E L T A O N A S
A T L B I G B A D J O L A Y
A Q A A A C R R G A O Y R D
A B N D N X O O X O Z X B N
R L J A I A A B J G Z O M A
B D A Q S D R I A O O T A X
M I H H T F Y A N S K A T N
A A Y D A A I V O I T L P A
V B V H L D D U A T O A E P
O E P O A Z Y Z R R B T S R
N F V W F R H Z Y A R A A I
K A L A N D R I E Q A E O L
C Z D T A S A B O T S Y P Y
```

APRILY
AOGOSITRA
KALANDRIE
FEBROARY
ZOMA
JANOARY
JOLAY
DIABE
ALATSINAINY

VOLANA
NOVAMBRA
OKTOBRA
ASABOTSY
SEPTAMBRA
ALAHADY
TALATA
ALAROBIA
TAONA

8 - Energy

```
L A S A N T S Y W J S A K E
G I N J E N I E F O V V A N
Z V F E L M X H H X J X R T
A Z O H A V A O Z I N A B R
N I F T O Y C H F D O R O O
O M R N R A C A A I T T N P
T A K E T A L F N E O A I Y
E O S N T S U A D S H R N R
P T F I Z A L N O E P A A A
D E D B A N B A T L Z N R E
B R P R M I S N O M Y I J L
W A K U S R F A A Q A R T K
U B G T V O Z B N I N E G O
R I V O T R A O A X H H T N
```

BATERIA	ORINASA
KARBONINA	MAOTERA
DIESEL	NOKLEARY
HERINARATRA	PHOTON
INJENIE	FANDOTOANA
ENTROPY	AZO HAVAOZINA
FEL	ETONA
LASANTSY	TURBINE
HAFANANA	RIVOTRA

9 - Archeology

```
F  F  A  N  A  D  I  H  A  D  I  A  N  A
Y  A  M  A  N  C  R  E  Z  T  Z  N  M  N
Z  N  H  P  D  N  D  K  L  O  A  A  H  I
U  A  R  I  I  M  X  I  J  M  V  S  P  F
Y  L  Z  O  N  K  M  P  R  B  A  A  R  A
L  O  X  Z  T  Y  A  A  X  A  T  F  O  I
O  A  K  O  K  A  V  R  W  N  R  Ô  F  M
P  T  C  V  X  U  N  J  O  A  A  S  E  A
M  O  K  K  G  J  G  X  O  K  Y  I  S  V
E  V  X  L  K  F  L  V  L  J  A  L  O  A
T  S  Y  F  A  N  T  A  T  R  A  Y  R  Z
R  O  E  V  J  X  L  V  D  I  Z  N  A  C
J  F  R  T  A  O  N  A  S  F  X  F  U  O
T  X  A  B  W  Y  N  A  J  A  N  X  A  B
```

FANADIHADIANA   PROFESORA
FAHINY   VAKOKA
TAOLANA   MPIKAROKA
ERA   EKIPA
TOMBANA   TEMPOLY
FÔSILY   FASANA
ZAVA-MIAFINA   TSY FANTATRA
ZAVATRA   TAONA

10 - Food #2

```
B H H E D P M F S A N J Z Y
B A O W R A C R S E K W D L
R I R O F O M O Ô W R O M G
O R D A Q M A M K D Y I H M
C E N R N A H A Ô X O F Z O
C L O T B J N Z L U G S V Y
O E R A W M E Y À K U E O A
L S T L R A Y L V I R H P G
I B F O Z R P U Y W T M V W
G V Z H W I H B H I L J W H
O R D N O K A S T T P G U C
Z V P O L A O V P K I H F W
M Q V O A T A B I A Z Y Z D
V A R Y A T O D Y O X N A K
```

PAOMA	ATODY
ARIKA	BARANJELY
AKONDRO	TRONDRO
MOFO	VOALOP
BROCCOLI	HAM
SELERIA	KIWI
FROMAZY	HOLATRA
SERIZY	VOATABIA
AKOHO	VARY
SÔKÔLÀ	YOGURT

11 - Chemistry

```
Y U S O L J E H T K A M R A
A G L I P Y L A T E M O A N
N S I W R A E G L H H L N Z
I K I B C A K N A A U E O I
N E A D G F T I N F N K N M
E R N D R L R S J A K I J A
Z O I I P A O T A N N O A O
I L N M L E N O I A O L V R
S H O N E A I K G N K A A G
K C B T E D K S A A L B T A
O X R J D H A L E X E Q R N
V F A N O I T R A R A L A I
T A K A T O M I K A R L W K
N Z D E N È G O R D Y H Y A
```

ASIDRA	ION
ALKALINE	RANON-JAVATRA
ATOMIKA	METALY
KARBONINA	MOLEKIOLA
FANOITRA	NOKLEARY
CHLORE	ORGANIKA
ELEKTRONIKA	OKSIZENINA
SINGA	SIRA
ANZIMA	HAFANANA
HYDROGÈNE	LANJA

12 - Music

```
T K I L A S I K A C A L M B
O O F I R I N D R A N A K U
T A N A R E D I F Z Z F T J
V O A O P M E T L O R M Y T
C B N Y N Z U M P I H I R A
R H U O P K O P É R A F M N
A L O O N D A L L A B I I O
K X L R D U M L N H B T K D
I I M D U J R M O I Z A R A
K Z C P X S H L L R N O Ô G
I M T M M G Y P L A U V H N
R N C C R I T F P F S A H K
A T K C T P H E B X B N L I
M O Z I K A M O U Q P A Z B
```

RAKIKIRA	MOZIKA
BALLAD	OPÉRA
CHORUS	TONONKALO
KILASIKA	RHYTHM
FIRINDRANA	NGADONA
FITAOVANA	HIRA
TONON	MPIHIRA
FIDERANA	TEMPO
MIKRÔ	FEO

13 - Family

```
M V D A D A T O A U L M Q U
N P A N I R E T A P I B E J
E V I V R A Z A M B E O G D
N A C R Y N I L E K I F A Z
I D Y H A L I H E L V N T F
T Y F E G Y V A V A H A R A
O R A Y D Q T P S L Z R A H
A Y L E K I F A Z T A A N A
R C Y Y Y N X S M Z Z H K Z
E M N A S Y E P S P A A I A
N D A D A B E P H O O L Z Z
Y L E P L R B X H O X A Y A
X B O H Y K E Y S E E H J N
A E O S G J B S E N W Y V A
```

RAZAMBE	DADABE
NENITOA	BEBE
RAHALAHY	ZAFIKELINY
ZAZA	LEHILAHY
FAHAZAZANA	RENY
ANKIZY	NEPHEW
MPIRAY TAM-PO	PATERINA
VAVY	RAHAVAVY
RAY	DADATOA
ZAFIKELY	VADY

14 - Farm #1

```
S K G N F N V C A V L X T J
O H O K A V O R Z B O G H W
A I G Q M A A O E E M P Q M
V E R J B P B W Z T B R N I
A V J W O A M H I S I A Q F
L J X Y L S N V K A D N W E
Y R A V E B A J A B I O R F
A W Y A N S L H A E A Y O Y
H O I V A K I L A Y A L S O
O M B I L A H Y K E L Y Y F
M C I B S E T A N T E L Y H
C G I M N V Y V J J E F D T
X Q I O F W S A K A Y Y L D
E D T R R S P D R X N D W K
```

FAMBOLENA   FEFY
BETSABE   ZEZIKA
OMBIDIA   SAHA
OMBILAHY KELY   OSY
SAKA   HAY
AKOHO   TANTELY
OMBIVAVY   SOAVALY
CROW   VARY
ALIKA   VOA
ANJAY   RANO

15 - Camping

```
W C J L A E O H B A M B Z F
A R A T N A T A R T E O T I
K D Y D A T D Z Z E G Z F T
O O M N K F Y A L R L A A A
R U M P A K O J W U E H R O
T Z Q P L L F I T T P H I V
A E Q Y À S J K F N I R H A
S F F A N A L A Z E J F Y N
V I L Z P P F Z H V A L A A
O T I N S E C T T D B X I O
L R P N C N H M M A P I H E
A A P U W Y F K J Y X U B C
N Z Y V S U F X R J U C A Y
A C E T T G B Q S S B D C G
```

ADVENTURE	INSECT
BIBY	FARIHY
EFITRA	FANALA
LAKANA	MAP
KOMPÀ	VOLANA
FITAOVANA	TOETRA
AFO	TADY
ALA	TANTARA
SATROKA	LAY
HAZA	HAZO

16 - Cats

```
T  W  H  Y  H  E  F  O  K  Q  D  C  Y  E
S  W  X  H  L  W  R  I  K  V  S  I  W  T
V  A  N  E  T  O  E  L  A  H  A  M  A  O
L  P  R  M  J  R  Z  U  W  C  Y  G  L  E
B  O  L  O  S  A  M  I  R  O  T  P  C  T
E  U  D  H  K  D  K  A  D  A  L  A  R  R
E  H  L  I  Z  E  Y  N  O  B  M  A  R  A
Y  N  W  P  R  O  N  J  X  S  K  W  E  Z
M  K  E  M  X  L  O  A  T  Y  T  E  I  L
J  S  E  A  Q  Y  L  N  T  P  C  A  L  J
X  I  W  M  X  L  O  A  R  R  X  V  M  Y
H  U  N  T  E  R  V  I  J  P  A  G  O  Q
T  O  T  O  Z  Y  L  L  Q  J  I  F  R  U
A  Y  C  F  O  T  C  I  D  C  L  A  D  M
```

CLAW	TOTOZY
ADALA	PAW
LIANA	TOETRA
MAMPIHOMEHY	SARO-KENATRA
VOLONY	TORIMASO
HUNTER	RAMBONY
MAHALEOTENA	DIA
KELY	KOFEHY

17 - Algebra

```
M B L V M G M K T W L N D A
V N W U O Z C I F S Y F I O
F A S I Z L G S Q H O U S T
O A H V H X A A R I M T O R
R N M A W H E R R T A N R A
M T A N O N P Y Y N N M B A
U O T A Y L L I N E A R Z G
L N R L H X A I A N G T W L
A Y I O P Q J N H O N X Y S
C P X I V Y Z N A P O X Z M
K G P C X W A R P X N O X I
G U H A P N O H M E A V A O
B E J K L T L T A Z F L W V
Y L P B S Y R F F S L P B A
```

KISARY	ISA
MIRA	OLANA
EXPONENT	BE
ANTONY	TSOTRA
DISO	VAHAOLANA
FORMULA	FANONGANA
AMPAHANY	VOLA
LINEAR	MIOVA
MATRIX	AOTRA

18 - Spices

```
L A V A N I L A A Y V C R L
L S H Z Y L H N N H X H O G
M A R I S C T O N G O L O O
A K T A N I L E N A K S B G
N A K Y S A G O L O G N O T
G M C U R R Y C V G Y L R C
I A K E E R G U N E F I M A
D L P A P R I K A M A C A R
Y A N O R F A S K T R O M D
A H N T S B V L T U D R Y A
J O T I S E Y D F N T I Y M
K B H I M I H V Z Q R C E O
E Z P Q D O R L E N N E F M
Y F T X P D K O J N I T S C
```

MANGIDY	TONGOLO GASY
CARDAMOM	SAKAMALAHO
KANELINA	LICORICE
CLOVE	NUTMEG
DRAFY	TONGOLO
KOMINA	PAPRIKA
CURRY	SAFRONA
FENNEL	SIRA
FENUGREEK	MAMY
TSIRO	LAVANILA

19 - Universe

```
A S T E R O I D O O T T C I
H L A T I T U D E R L U D V
I A S T R O N O M A B B J O
T A T M O S F É R A T I P L
A Y G A L A X Y A G V D T A
M R E K O A T E R A U S E N
A A E Y L A I T S E L E S A
S O N C Q A Z O D I A K A G
O W O I W Y N A T N A L O B
M V E M Z V P I U W U N F U
S O L S T I C E T S Z T D F
W O C O A I A A B R A L O S
X J G C H P D H G V A G B T
C H O R I Z O N S K S B C O
```

ASTEROID	HORIZON
ASTRONOMA	LATITUDE
ATMOSFÉRA	VOLANA
SELESTIALY	ORBIT
COSMIC	LANITRA
HAIZINA	SOLAR
EON	SOLSTICE
EKOATERA	ARY
GALAXY	HITA MASO
BOLANTANY	ZODIAKA

20 - Mammals

```
S L G N C B G H C I E L O Y
O R U P Q I I B Z V T D V R
A K A J Q T D X Q Z O M B Y
V N A J S R R F O X Y H P F
A E O N A O O K E J O O P A
L I C I G K B E R A C T E R
Y A K I L A O N Y S Z R L I
F E E O Q U R B Q A E O E Z
E A N O J H E O A K B Z F L
S J K B I E V B O A R O A P
O P W S L V A D J M A N N W
G X R G I Z E O Z S E A T A
Z Z X R G I B L A M S W A Z
B N N W O L F O N D R Y E J
```

BERA	RAJAKO
BEAVER	SOAVALY
OMBY	KANGAROO
SAKA	LIONA
COYOTE	GIDRO
ALIKA	BITRO
FESO	ONDRY
ELEFANTA	TROZONA
FOX	WOLF
ZIRAFY	ZEBRA

21 - Fishing

```
I P R K V A N Z C H N R E T
V J F U N O B M A S O M H O
O S E A N A M K Y J O O X R
C L L X N S P B R A N O K A
O L A K A N A V O A T I F P
O I N A R T A T I N A M Q A
K G J T Y O I N F A Y V O S
J M A V X X D X J T H H N I
R E N I R A N O O E I A S K
U W V H Q X G Y N R R R Y A
G C K Q W Z K X O A A O S L
O F E W L V B M J H F N R G
E A H T R V F D D A R A X Y
M U W I O M Y O W F J A W N
```

JONO	HOOK
HARONA	JAW
TORAPASIKA	FARIHY
SAMBO	OSEANA
COOK	FAHARETANA
FITAOVANA	RENIRANO
MANITATRA	RANO
VOMBONY	LANJA
GILLS	

22 - Restaurant #1

```
I  J  K  S  Q  N  X  S  H  W  O  F  U  M
F  A  N  G  A  R  O  A  A  A  C  D  M  S
F  Q  N  O  M  O  H  K  N  I  B  Z  G  J
K  E  Q  K  X  X  O  A  A  T  U  A  S  H
M  C  P  K  Y  C  K  F  H  R  W  I  O  U
H  E  N  A  N  F  A  O  I  E  A  Q  R  X
A  L  E  R  J  I  A  T  R  S  K  B  E  C
A  N  T  S  Y  U  K  B  D  S  A  C  I  G
T  O  L  O  T  R  A  P  N  T  K  T  H  L
B  F  J  M  O  Q  T  C  A  S  A  O  S  Y
T  O  K  A  F  E  V  V  M  N  I  G  A  E
L  M  H  D  O  D  A  C  A  S  S  K  C  R
L  A  K  O  Z  I  A  A  F  Q  A  J  R  S
Y  T  Z  J  H  N  M  N  M  P  M  G  Z  H
```

ALERJIA	ANTSY
MOFO	HENA
CASHIER	TOLOTRA
AKOHO	NAPKIN
KAFE	FAMANDRIHANA
SAKAFO	SAOSY
FANGARO	MASIAKA
LAKOZIA	WAITRESS

23 - Bees

```
S Z A V A M A N I R Y N I S
Z A M Q G T Q N C O N I N A
A X K A R T O H O T O V S M
R M T A H J Y T U A B A E I
I X A K F A B Z G N O N C H
D O N O W O S N E I V G T A
A Z T R R R O O B L O O C F
I A E T W D J E A L V N Z A
N K L E N N K Y S O N G E B
A N Y S T A P D D P O O L A
D I U X Z O S A V O K A A A
Z N P X I S Y P U Y O L T W
V O A N K A Z O M U T N R R
R V H Q D M L Q E J W R A M
```

MAHASOA
SAMIHAFA
VONINKAZO
SAKAFO
VOANKAZO
ZARIDAINA
TOHOTRA
TANTELY
INSECT

ZAVAMANIRY
VOVOBONY
POLLINATOR
SETROKA
MASOANDRO
NIVANGONGO
SAVOKA
ELATRA

24 - Photography

```
F H M Q I Y J M N M U M I Z
T A A Y T N I A M A L I X A
B K M W H D R H Y S Y F X V
L C D P N A O W T O R A X A
S O T M I K I A B P A N A T
Z Z K Y D R W Z M E S O N R
A A Q O U T A E I M T H A A
V K L S Y Q W N K N N I T S
U Q Q M E S Z Q T T A T I I
E N D R I K A T I I K R R F
S E J H M Q X C H J A A A R
Y R E J I F A B M O F N M A
M I H A S I M B A K O L A M
O E Z P O R T R A I T I F E
```

MAINTY	FRAME
FAKANTSARY	JIRO
LOKO	ZAVATRA
MIFANOHITRA	FOMBA FIJERY
HAIZINA	PORTRAIT
FAMARITANA	ALOKA
FAMPIRANTIANA	MIHASIMBA
ENDRIKA	MASO

25 - Weather

```
C T H A N A F A M Y N A T H
H E L A T R A M A I N A O A
Z G Z F V T S Z Y X A K R I
G P P P I A Z F O E R E N N
R Y S C R R E D G D T G A T
X A N A V A M O R N O V D A
P T H M I V I Y Y V V V O N
P E C O U J G O J X I B I Y
M Y R D N A M O N A R H B R
R I Z N F A R C L Y D U O I
A N A N I A I P O V I R R Y
L A N I T R A N A N A F A H
O T O E T R A N D R O M N W
P W N A T Z A V O N A R A A
```

RIVO-PIAINANA
TOETRANDRO
RAHONA
HAIN-TANY
MAINA
ZAVONA
RIVO-DOZA
RANOMANDRY
HELATRA

ORANA
POLAR
AVANA
LANITRA
DRIVOTRA
HAFANANA
VARATRA
TORNADO
TANY MAFANA

26 - Adventure

```
F  H  A  T  S  A  R  A  T  A  R  E  H  Y
H  A  T  O  E  R  A  N  A  A  F  D  W  F
A  R  H  V  W  N  Y  J  S  I  A  Q  I
F  T  F  A  D  A  A  A  F  A  F  Z  B  T
A  E  I  N  S  G  H  I  L  N  A  O  C  S
N  O  A  A  E  A  O  Y  M  A  L  D  E  A
A  T  R  N  M  G  R  N  V  H  I  I  V  K
M  V  O  A  W  A  A  O  H  A  A  D  A  A
P  B  V  M  B  H  K  P  T  F  N  I  O  N
O  T  A  O  Y  A  I  M  U  A  A  P  V  A
P  W  N  I  B  M  F  I  M  H  N  M  A  N
Z  K  A  F  W  C  D  R  F  A  N  A  O  A
N  A  M  A  N  A  U  E  M  F  N  N  H  Y
J  A  R  T  A  Z  A  H  A  M  Y  S  T  T
```

ASA	FIFALIANA
HATSARATAREHY	TOETRA
HERIM-PONY	FIKAROHANA
NAMPIDI-DOZA	VAOVAO
TOERANA	FAHAFAHANA
FAHASAROTANA	FIOMANANA
HAFANAM-PO	FIAROVANA
FITSAKANANA	MAHAGAGA
NAMANA	TSY MAHAZATRA

27 - Circus

```
M P F C E H R G C G V M J M
A N O I L O N N I C E J U O
H B C L S O Y V K D Q F G Z
A I Y M A M O T A V R Q G I
T Z D N R N C Q I B N O L K
A H O N G Y I B T D I Q E A
L F Y J I C F N V T U B R T
A I K O T C F A O H E S Y N
N T Y J J N P O L A P F M A
J A Q N Q U S M Y A L N D F
O K Z A L I K A P A T A Y E
N A A K K V N T A H G Y B L
A D O A Q V O S Z W L Y T E
B T U G T A B O R C A U G Z
```

ACROBAT	GIDRO
BIBY	MOZIKA
BALAONINA	MATSO
VATOMAMY	SEHO
AKANJO	MAHATALANJONA
ELEFANTA	LAY
VOLY	TAPAKILA
JUGGLER	TIGRA
LIONA	FITAKA
ODY	

28 - Tools

```
T X E G X J I P N Q E S V F
T A E O G V C A B L E T H A
M O N N Y I A N T S Y A O N
C P H T D S R E I L P P W I
A Y I A A Y B R N R J L S L
I A E T T N E Y Y H L E B O
S Q X E O R A Z L D Q R C D
V N L L E N A N O N W C V I
B X U L I W D M A Z E R A H
G A R A D N P R K A Z G H W
N H B M A N A R A I D O K E
F L K I N W Y T L Z H E T Y
K E N X D J M N S G M Z M H
D B V V N B D J T L Y E V F
```

AX	HAREZA
CABLE	TADY
LAKAOLY	MPITONDRA
TANTANANA	HETY
ANTSY	VISY
TOHATRA	STAPLER
MALLET	FANILO
PLIERS	KODIARANA

29 - Restaurant #2

```
M A N S L E G I O M A Q M V
A Z E S O Q O A A F Z V B O
C P Z A V A M A N I T R A A
A Z P R A N O M A N D R Y N
K A P E A S E R V E R A D K
E V A F T T Y T J E R I A A
H A T O O I O P G O A Z L Z
X P Y Q S R Z D R B N I A O
G I A B H N K E Y S O N S R
B S L A S O P Y R I W K O T
W O T R O N D R O R B S U O
J T V G J E B W A A P G I S
P R M A T S I R O H I T G X
N O S A K A F O H A R I V A
```

APPETIZER
ZAVA-PISOTRO
CAKE
SEZA
MATSIRO
SAKAFO HARIVA
ATODY
TRONDRO
FORK
VOANKAZO

RANOMANDRY
PATY
SALADY
SIRA
LASOPY
ZAVA-MANITRA
SOTRO
LEGIOMA
SERVERA
RANO

30 - Geology

```
S V M O N A K L O V G K Q H
G D I I I J S X V G L R U O
R A N O S O S I N O O I A R
Y P E C Q J P D D I G S R O
I L R S O Y R N T R S T T H
O T A V R R L L H F A A Z O
B U L R A A A M E R M L Q R
R V Y S I X Q L V I O Y F O
I H J I Q S O F A A I H Ô N
G E Y S E R N K M K S O S T
P L A T E A U A V A L Z I A
S T A L A C T I T E A Y L N
A T N A N I T N O A K T Y Y
T S I N G E R I N A H N Z X
```

ASIDRA   GEYSER
KALSIOMA   LAVA
ZOHY   SOSONA
KAONTINANTA   MINERALY
CORAL   PLATEAU
KRISTALY   QUARTZ
TSINGERINA   SIRA
HOROHORONTANY   STALACTITE
RIAKA   VATO
FÔSILY   VOLKANO

31 - House

```
F T A F A N A L A H I D Y R
I V R M G O W Z M G Y K R I
K A T Z P N E F Z C O H E N
A R A Z Y A L E P H I T T D
N A R S C R T G M H K A H R
D V A K S T P A T R Z N A I
R A T I L I L R N A Q Y T N
A R I F S F A A T A F G L A
N A F A W E W G K N R O Q J
A N H F F M G A G O L A E J
M A N A O R D N A F Z Q A I
X O Z A R I D A I N A I L R
E G O Y F E F A N A K A A O
A M B A N Y R I H A N A H H
```

AMBANY RIHANA
KIFAFA
LAY
VARAVARANA
FEFY
AM-PATANA
TANY
FANAKA
GARAGE
ZARIDAINA

FANALAHIDY
LAKOZIA
JIRO
TAHTERY
FITARATRA
TAFO
EFITRANO
FANDROANA
RINDRINA
FIKANDRANA

32 - Physics

```
H A I H E T S I K A Y F X I
H H R S F V E L O M A A N N
T A H I O O G N I A H N C J
S S K X W M R A K C O A M E
I E A I X I B M S Q C N A N
V M N O T F A I U Y A D G I
A A A R Y R L F N L N R N E
K L R G I I O H F Y A A E D
Y E A C V L I K K A G M T J
H A T E T I K A Y O N A I I
K Q I C S I E V D Y I N S A
V X N O M Y L U W G A A M T
Y R A E L K O N G P H E A K
T J F U F A M S I M I K A H
```

HAINGANA
TSIVAKY
SIMIKA
HAKITROKY
INJENIE
FANITARANA
FANANDRAMANA
FORMULA
HATETIKA

MAGNETISM
LAMESA
HAIHETSIKA
MOLEKIOLA
NOKLEARY
SOMBINY
HAINGO
VELOMA

33 - Dance

```
K N F B A Q L R F M U N W K
D O G I O S Q M A O E Z Y O
O T L D H J L U K Z T G E R
F N U O A E N C I I A M F E
I A U Z N X T T S K I G G O
H K Z J A T N S T A M A F G
E B D M N M S O E X E S K R
T C P E E P A A H H D R U A
S Z E J R N S S I G A D J F
I P X C E Q E J O N K M J I
K F W O M H T Y H R A R P A
A N A S A I M A R A I P M O
S T N L F L M V A T A N A V
K I L A S I K A L A H K L N
```

AKADEMIA   HETSIKA
KANTO   MOZIKA
VATANA   MPIARA-MIASA
KOREOGRAFIA   FIHETSIKA
KILASIKA   FAMERENANA
KOLONTSAINA   RHYTHM
FIHETSEHAM-PO   MASO

34 - Coffee

```
Z B R Z R W B K Z S E K U R
P A T R G X P A E L T G Z O
K K V R T J B F L S S U R N
B A N A V I S E Y K I S T O
M O N W P E C I R P R I X N
A P M Y D I G N A M O R Q O
S A X A N F S A G W N A B F
I K K T I U I O R N A M A E
D C U N R N R A T N R A W M
R Z M Z G J T E V R W M O B
A N A Q I Q U Y R I O Y R A
M A R A I N A Z O B A A R U
U Z U A U A R T O S O N A F
M X A R T A V A J N O N A R
```

ASIDRA
ZAVA-PISOTRO
MANGIDY
MAINTY
KAFEINA
FANOSOTRA
KAPOAKA
SIVANA
TSIRO

GRIND
RANON-JAVATRA
RONONO
MARAINA
FIAVIANA
PRICE
SIRAMAMY
RANO

35 - Colors

```
I N D I G O R M D M H K U Q
B Y A A Z U R E A E E E P P
E Z N Y T N I A M I Y N Q M
I Q V U C A W G S Z T D A A
G A I M A G E N T A F S V V
E U O B R O W N T I S V O O
I X L F U C H S I A E O N K
K Y E M A N G A R E P A Q E
Y S T O F G R A Y U I S S L
M A V O H A A Z V H A A Z Y
J O F X M H C C E L P R U P
N O W D V L L V U U C Y T I
I Q P W W W F Z A A Z J X R
I C N S D O F B Z E F S Q T
```

AZURE   MAGENTA
BEIGE   VOASARY
MAINTY   MAVOKELY
MANGA   PURPLE
BROWN   MENA
CYAN   SEPIA
FUCHSIA   VIOLET
MAITSO   FOTSY
GRAY   MAVO
INDIGO

36 - Shapes

```
H X L Q B A P C R A B H T G
Y N I S I S R O S D T N E A
P X M Y C Q I R L I W B L T
E V R U C O S N M M D A O S
R S C W K F M E W A Q N Z T
B K P A R L S R J R K D O H
O W P I Q S N S L I P A R N
L A S Y L L C A I P B L O I
A B O G U L H Z E D P A E E
S D A B X A E A P T E N V H
I N I R A G N I R A V A B Z
G R A N A L O B I R A F S Q
L J K D C C C M A H I T S I
M A R O L A F Y F I I X M O
```

ARC   HYPERBOLA
FARIBOLANA   ANDALANA
CONE   MAROLAFY
CORNER   PRISM
GOBA   PIRAMIDA
CURVE   MAHITSI-
VARINGARIN'I   SIDE
SISINY   TELOZORO
ELLIPSE

37 - Scientific Disciplines

```
I  A  S  C  I  T  S  I  U  N  E  T  B  B
F  S  O  R  D  N  A  R  T  E  O  T  O  I
Y  T  S  A  Q  J  T  N  C  D  P  R  C  O
H  R  I  Y  G  O  L  A  R  E  N  I  M  C
A  O  O  T  R  H  K  Y  N  A  T  O  B  H
I  N  L  L  Z  G  W  Q  M  Y  Y  A  T  E
H  O  O  C  W  T  I  E  E  G  I  J  Z  M
E  M  J  Z  S  H  D  M  A  O  O  N  W  I
T  A  I  M  I  S  X  M  P  L  Y  A  D  S
S  U  A  A  Y  A  I  P  I  O  H  Y  G  T
I  H  A  I  A  I  N  A  L  C  J  S  F  R
K  I  Y  G  O  L  O  I  S  E  N  I  K  Y
A  O  Q  M  B  O  D  A  N  A  T  O  M  Y
F  I  S  I  O  L  O  J  I  A  C  Z  T  Z
```

ANATOMY	KINESIOLOGY
ASTRONOMA	TENUISTICS
BIOCHEMISTRY	HAIHETSIKA
HAIAINA	TOETRANDRO
BOTANY	MINERALOGY
SIMIA	FISIOLOJIA
ECOLOGY	SOSIOLOJIA
TANY	

38 - Science

```
T E V O L I S I O N A T P L
F S W F B J O Y K X A O E F
A G I T O P Y R Y X F E T A
N Z I V F Ô S I L Y I T R N
D A P H A O F N A S Z R A A
I Y C R L K D A R I Ì A K N
N V G K O M Y M E M K N E D
I T I D I D I A N A A D V R
H M A R K T R V I V N R I A
A R Y C E M S A M A N O T M
N T E F L P F Z R Z B T R A
A W I C O T O E T R A M A N
E U J P M S I M I K A S O A
L A B O R A T O A R A R K F
```

TSIVAKY
SIMIKA
TOETRANDRO
EVOLISIONA
FANANDRAMANA
ZAVA-MISY
FÔSILY
PETRA-KEVITRA
LABORATOARA

FOMBA
MINERALY
MOLEKIOLA
TOETRA
FANDINIHANA
POTI
FIZÌKA
ZAVAMANIRY

39 - Beauty

```
B T T R C S S T Y L I S T L
Y U I O O P H W N W R S S O
M Y W V Q N C A J A H E C K
F A R T O L O T M B N Y I O
A R K T Y X A L R P D U N M
H T F I N Y D G Y O O C E E
A A Q H A R T I D O H O G N
S K C A R Z L H J K I E O A
O O U N A X Y O Q O Y Z T D
A V R I S T M T B L S I O Y
V F L T T H A N I T R A H R
A F A R A C S A M D W F P T
N O F Y H J J K J H S Z N W
A F I T A R A T R A T Q W I
```

HATSARANY
LOKO
MAKIAZY
CURL
HAJA
KANTO
HANITRA
FAHASOAVANA
LOKOMENA
MASCARA

FITARATRA
PHOTOGENIC
VOKATRA
HANITRY
HETY
TOLOTRA
SHAMPOO
HODITRA
STYLIST

40 - To Fill

```
E M V P K P L W S I N Y K S
T A V O A H A N G Y I S H U
J V C R A T E I J R S O A I
L L U V I X H C X N A A N T
Q A G M V U A W A J B P D C
Q K H X O O R O J A F E R A
X I V A L R O P A T I K A S
R R W A T E N O T R A C N E
I A P C L A A N A S O N O F
T B P S D O H V A Z Y M S N
F A F F Z Z P I M C N V T Z
H R W K X L U Y R T T K N C
U U Z O S S S Z U Y M A A D
V A T A S A R I H A N A F D
```

KITAPO
BARIKA
BASIN
HARONA
TAVOAHANGY
EFAJORO
SINY
CARTON
CRATE

VATASARIHANA
VALOPY
LAHATAHIRY
FONOSANA
PAOSY
SUITCASE
LOVIA
FANTSONA
VAZY

41 - Clothes

```
K Y X X D E I C Z V B W O V
L A N A N A T N O N O F C K
X K P U M V E Z K P B M G A
A A N A R T I A R T I A H P
O B I K N I H E F A J Z J A
J O B O F Y K I R A R O E H
N L L R I H D H J E B J A O
A S O T R E S O Y O A O N L
K W U A A F W A A Z I R S A
A M S S V Z E T N M E Y L T
Y K E R A O A I O F A S P A
J Y H C K R T L R G V L Y P
X C L I A Y E A P V X B W M
X U Z F Q W R P A Y J Y F G
```

APRONA
FEHIN-KIBO
BLOUSE
HAITRAITRA
AKANJO
LAMAODY
FONON-TANANA
SATROKA
PALITAO
JEANS

FIRAVAKA
ROJO
PATALOHA
KAPA
FEHY
LOBAKA
KIRARO
ZIPO
KAPANY
SWEATER

42 - Insects

```
V O Q A P A R A S Y R V Y X
W A V R A L P K U C X O B J
F L L T E N R O H H K A E R
T A K A E Z G M K B M N T J
P L D Q L C U I X H C G S R
A A M O O A R Q D F F O A E
O K O D O I F A T I L R B L
L G L Y Z R D S W A N Y E L
O A Z Y B W H H B W Y A U Q
L D D T L A N A K N A K T H
M A B Y Z S I T N A M Y T Z
Y C Y O B P A P H I D Y X G
I I I Z D U T E R M I T E U
F C V Y N L G X Y B M J T K
```

TAFIO - DOKO
APHID
BETSABE
VOANGORY
LOLO
CICADA
KALALAO
ANGIDINA
PARASY

VALALA
HORNET
LADYBUG
LARVA
MANTIS
MOKA
TERMITE
WASP
KANKANA

43 - Astronomy

```
S Y R A O B A V A Z V O S A
A O O W K M G O Q Q R M O S
S L L J X J S L K D J L R T
T A Z A H A R A G K Q C A E
R N O R R T O N J A U F T R
O I D T W E E A Y C L H R O
N T I A C N T C Q V U A A I
O R A R P A E H S K J T X D
M A K A R L M I K U L F O Y
A H A T E P Z N K B P T N E
B A L A F O M A N G A A I C
M P A N A M O R Y N A N U Q
Z A N A B O L A N A S Y Q P
E C L I P S E H T Y C D E L
```

ASTEROID	NA
MPANAMORY	ZAVABOARY
ASTRONOMA	PLANETA
SORATRA	TARATRA
TANY	BALAFOMANGA
ECLIPSE	ZANABOLANA
EQUINOX	LANITRA
GALAXY	SOLAR
METEOR	RAHA
VOLANA	ZODIAKA

44 - Health and Wellness #2

```
A  N  I  T  E  R  A  H  I  E  M  Z  F  F
D  A  R  A  H  O  P  I  T  A  L  Y  A  A
I  N  O  I  T  S  E  G  I  D  X  S  N  H
N  A  S  A  L  A  M  A  S  S  L  J  O  A
T  T  N  L  Y  U  V  S  X  F  P  B  R  D
S  O  F  A  K  A  S  R  R  H  D  L  A  I
A  M  P  S  M  M  D  H  K  S  L  O  N  O
I  Y  W  E  A  E  A  L  D  O  H  O  A  V
N  E  I  R  O  L  A  K  A  M  M  M  F  A
A  A  N  A  R  T  I  S  Z  N  H  A  Q  N
O  U  N  A  L  E  R  J  I  A  J  D  N  A
V  I  T  A  M  I  N  I  N  A  U  A  M  A
A  N  G  O  V  O  S  A  M  I  R  O  T  P
F  O  T  O  T  A  R  A  Z  O  L  I  L  G
```

ALERJIA	SALAMA
ANATOMY	HOPITALY
KOMANA	FAHADIOVANA
RA	FANORANA
KALORIE	TOE-PO
SAKAFO	SITRANA
DIGESTION	TORIMASO
ARETINA	ADIN - TSAINA
ANGOVO	VITAMININA
FOTOTARAZO	LANJA

45 - Time

```
O L N Q H T A L O H A T X M
M E J G O O N X U M J S K I
A E V B R N A N I L A Y B N
L O T V D W N V O R A H A I
Y Y D D N X O K Y L F O N T
F O T O A N A T A R F E O R
F Y H C N C T A N I O L A A
Y N N A I R O A T O D A T J
U W V Q R K L Q X R Q S N A
D H X N E L O V O L A N A N
I H H M H M F J U F U S S D
T A O N J A T O M A R O I R
M A R A I N A T A O N A S O
C S K X J K A L A N D R I E
```

TAORIAN'NY
ISAN-TAONA
TALOHA
KALANDRIE
TAONJATO MARO
ANDRO
FOLO TAONA
HOAVY
ORA
MINITRA

FOTOANA
VOLANA
MARAINA
ALINA
TSY HO ELA
ANIO
HERINANDRO
TAONA
OMALY

46 - Buildings

```
B A R N O T H T G P Q F P S
N R K U B S O L E T S O H A
L H J Y L E T H Q A M Z S R
T A T L E K E D H K T A S I
O S B D M O L H X I Y R L M
E A K O K L Y P X A B T A A
T N Y N R Y M O B N C I H H
O I E A P A L O E J Z F O O
E R J R E L T M S A T E P Z
T O J T Q G T O D E M M I F
R Y R A O B A V A Z U K T H
A N H K E B N P Z R Y M A M
M A S O I V O H O T A E L V
C G X T I L I K A M B O Y R
```

TRANO	LABORATOARA
BARN	MOSEUM
EFITRA	ZAVABOARY
LAPA	SEKOLY
SARIMAHO	KIANJA
MASOIVOHO	TOETOETRA
NY ORINASA	LAY
HOPITALY	TEATRA
HOSTEL	TILIKAMBO
HOTELY	

47 - Herbalism

```
L A V E N D E R W S V M I C
K J Y W U G Y D S A O A L U
O M A R O J R A M F N N A L
Q J Z F A D V F F R I I I I
Y X C E G M I N T O N T N N
R X G N Y B E D F N K R A A
I N P N Z G Y S M A A A W R
N R S E F I V O O V Z M B Y
A M Z L T S I R O R O Y A P
M A I T S O N A G E R O S S
A Z A R I D A I N A G J I A
V T O N G O L O G A S Y L Y
A A Q P S T I P E R S I L Y
Z E U J M A H A S O A K I T
```

MANITRA	ILAINA
BASIL	LAVENDER
MAHASOA	MARJORAM
CULINARY	MINT
FENNEL	OREGANO
TSIRO	PERSILY
VONINKAZO	ZAVAMANIRY
ZARIDAINA	ROSEMARY
TONGOLO GASY	SAFRONA
MAITSO	

48 - Vehicles

```
K O D I A R A N A E P W X T
N R T H P E D Y A N F B P Q
T T E O J T E B I V B A K A
C E K W C O B M A S A M R F
Q M J A A O X I Z M M R C F
O D L W R C H D B A I I A Z
X C R X P S J I O O V N D C
K A M I A O F G U T E J O M
J T E K D A R N Z E Z E E X
D A V A N Q O A P R I N J V
G X E Y H M T E F A V I L C
J I N W Y S C F Z T E E X F
A E I N I K T M A L Z K K C
B I S I K I L E T A Y R Q L
```

BISIKILETA
SAMBO
CAR
CARAVAN
INJENIE
BAKA
ANGIDIMBY
MAOTERA
RAFT

SCOOTER
MIVEZIVEZY
METRO
TAXI
KODIARANA
TCTOR
KAMIAO
VAN

49 - Flowers

```
P Y L B G P C M G D D F M D
L H A G C A U C X A P X A J
U I V X R R R H P I C P G A
M B E R K C K D I S D O N S
E I N O B Y N Z E Y R P O M
R S D S Z L V A C N D P L I
I C E E S D I K R O I Y I N
A U R L W Z W L C E Q A A E
M S G C A L I L Y T U L I P
N V M L H Y D A F F O D I L
R E W O L F N O I S S A P A
K C Z V M I T O X H W R P T
N S S E N O I L E D N A D E
O M S R U Q D C L P R C P P
```

CLOVER   MAGNOLIA
DAFFODIL   ORKID
DAISY   PASSIONFLOWER
DANDELION   PEONY
GARDENIA   PETAL
HIBISCUS   PLUMERIA
JASMINE   POPPY
LAVENDER   ROSE
LILAC   TULIP
LILY

50 - Health and Wellness #1

```
F  H  A  N  O  A  N  A  N  A  H  N  F  T
S  I  R  S  R  X  P  K  K  I  O  H  A  A
T  F  A  Q  C  A  E  I  U  R  Z  O  N  O
A  A  N  L  K  N  T  Q  P  E  A  R  A  L
P  H  A  S  A  I  M  R  Z  T  T  M  F  A
A  A  O  V  R  M  A  Y  A  K  R  O  O  N
K  Z  B  R  E  T  B  N  O  A  A  N  D  A
A  A  A  R  T  I  D  O  H  B  V  I  Y  V
Z  R  S  F  O  D  V  V  L  R  I  N  T  I
L  A  T  Z  K  Q  Q  A  I  Y  R  A  M  L
E  N  I  V  O  E  T  H  H  U  O  X  X  O
F  A  F  R  D  A  J  A  Y  H  S  J  F  S
L  E  V  I  T  R  A  H  D  N  Y  N  T  K
J  Y  O  F  L  F  I  H  E  T  S  I  K  A
```

MIASA	RATRA
BAKTERIA	FANAFODY
TAOLANA	HOZATRA
DOKOTERA	LEVITRA
TAPAKA	FIHETSIKA
FAHAZARANA	FIALAM-BOLY
HAHAVONY	HODITRA
HORMONINA	FITSABOANA
HANOANANA	VIROSY

51 - Town

```
T O F O M A V O A N A F D S
A F K I K A X P T S E N A E
H L I I V S A L O N Z N P K
T O B S A A Y L E T O H J O
E R A G R N R S E F A C G L
R I N H Q C J O I V L P D Y
Y S K S M S P A T P I C Y N
U T V N U P A R T A E T J F
O N I V E R S I T E N W R E
O O I D S H G C C D K A W A
Z D J E O T O E T O E T R A
Q N X Y M G A L L E R Y F W
M Q E W S A R I M A H O D H
A U M E X G J G I K F C O L
```

FANAOVA-MOFO	LEVITRA
BANK	SALON
CAFE	SEKOLY
SARIMAHO	KIANJA
FLORIST	FIVAROTANA
GALLERY	TOETOETRA
HOTELY	TEATRA
TAHTERY	ONIVERSITE
TSENA	ZOO
MOSEUM	

52 - Antarctica

```
F I T R A N D R A H A N A Y
D Z U W B T S X V J G O L P
N U I T C A K O R A K I P M
Q R W A R T O V I R T O J A
S A I K I N O S Y R Z Y D L
R I H I R A K V L A J H I O
A F A F A N N O A N B P A T
H A F I N I O R R O D A E A
O R A T O T S O E M O R F V
N G N N N N Y N N A Z G U V
A O A A B O E A I N C O V E
S E N I Q A O V M D H P L R
W J A S D K L I A R O O V P
T R O Z O N A S N Y W T L A
```

BAY	MINERALY
VORONA	SAIKINOSY
RAHONA	MPIKAROKA
KAONTINANTA	VATOLAMPY
COVE	SIANTIFIKA
DIA	HAFANANA
FITRANDRAHANA	TOPOGRAPHY
JEOGRAFIA	RANO
RANOMANDRY	TROZONA
NOSY	RIVOTRA

53 - Ballet

```
M W U I T F M K H T S K Z B
I A N U E I P O O E O Q Q A
M J F Q H H I R Z K L C K L
P J E Y A E H E A N O T F L
O D H E K T A O T I O L D E
T R B N A S I G R K U J N R
N R K P J I N R A A L L M I
A H F E E K O A N O S E L N
K Y U O S A Y F E Z D S K A
D T B Z M I A I A Y Q K T D
E H F B B B T A R E O A W N
J M H W C B A R M O Z I K A
M P A N D I H Y A S J B A R
F A M E R E N A N A X A N U
```

TEHAKA
KANTO
MPIHAINO
BALLERINA
KOREOGRAFIA
MPANDIHY
FIHETSIKA
MAFY
LESONA

HOZATRA
MOZIKA
ORKESITRA
FAMERENANA
RHYTHM
SOLO
FOMBA
TEKNIKA

54 - Fashion

```
I C J F T S O T R A A O M I
K V Y I X G T E Y N I R M A
X G U R N F N U X A N I A N
D J D O L E A Q X I A G L A
X A X N Z Y K I Q F N I A S
L R U A R M M T R A Z N F E
W A M N I W A U O T V A O F
I D M A X C A O T I X L N E
C A F B B R X B D F H C B R
F R N T A A N I L E T N A D
T O D Y A W I I A Z R H M N
A B M I S A H I M D M I O A
A M U B V E R K U J W M N F
I A N B A R T O K O B Z K A
```

BOUTIQUE
BOKOTRA
FITAFIANA
AINA
KANTO
AMBORADARA
LAFO
LAMBA

DANTELINA
FANDREFESANA
MAODERINA
TSOTRA
ORIGINAL
FOMBA
MIHASIMBA
FIRONANA

55 - Human Body

```
F V L Q T A N A N A S R H N
T I V A A N K L E J J L O J
U U T P J C S E C A D Z D M
F X G K R W O L O H A L I H
J X U W A J F F F O R O T L
C H I N R H I B H D T H R R
V A V A T I N P C I A A A P
Q G Y A O P A A E T O L I R
I T W G G K C B S A L I H B
W C K F N T W G M T A K A Z
V X I A O S E Z X S N A O U
K C H P T G J N V R A A T O
Y N O R O S H J A F V G R A
O R O N A T E N D A W F I Q
```

ANKLE	LOHA
RA	FO
TAOLANA	JAW
ATIDOHA	LOHALIKA
CHIN	TONGOTRA
SOFINA	VAVA
KIHO	TENDA
TENA	ORONA
RANTSAN-	SORONY
TANANA	HODITRA

56 - Musical Instruments

```
D E M E G T R P C R R A R V
O N A I P U X A P S F K D P
S O R Y P E R C U S S I O N
A B I A R A T I G A Y T J O
X M M X A W T N F M D R N O
O O B S H Y Z O W P K O A S
P R A G O N G M U O O M B S
H T Q Z F J G R H N B P Q A
O C H I M E S A L G O E W B
N D N I J J C H N A E T N K
E Y Q M A N D O L I N R C C
T A M B O U R I N E D A R K
L O K A N G A B E M B O W G
K V S L O K A N G A O A S X
```

BANJO	MANDOLIN
BASSOON	MARIMBA
LOKANGABE	OBOE
CHIMES	PERCUSSION
AMPONGA	PIANO
SODINA	SAXOPHONE
GONG	TAMBOURINE
GITARA	TROMBONE
HARMONICA	TROMPETRA
HARP	LOKANGA

57 - Cooking Tools

```
B K Q O Q X I U R K Y S M U
I U P M G R A T E R F T P T
V X N N B B L V X O D R A O
L S N F O U L D V F S A N A
W Y M Y R F M E A Z D I A S
M O J B O M L Q N I Y N K T
C I J M A B S Z A D J E O E
A O E C F N U U T K E R I R
K R L B A L T R A U Z R T W
N T I A L Z P S F Q H F R H
M O R E N A Y Y Y T O X A E
F S T Q F D S P A T U L A T
J U I C E R E L T T E K B Y
L T N P J X Y R E L T U C I
```

BLENDER	LAFAORO
COLANDER	HETY
CUTLERY	SPATULA
FORK	SOTRO
GRATER	FATANA
JUICER	STRAINER
KETTLE	MPANAKOITRA
ANTSY	TOASTER

58 - Fruit

```
S J C B E R R Y B X P E R O
H E H P C P O F V X C V P O
R Y R R E B P S A R N Y T C
Y L V I Z B V O A S A R Y A
E D X R Z E P Z K A V I L P
M B X O Z Y A P A P Z P P R
M A C F K V M T E U G A A I
A H N U Y A K O V A Z I O C
N R T G N O O F Q S O S M O
A Y A V A G U K I W I O A T
N V O O R D N O K A N T C T
A T S I P F O V A T A O V L
S N E C T A R I N E O C W J
Y V O A L O P V I C V H U P
```

PAOMA	KIWI
APRICOT	MANGA
ZAVOKA	VOATAVO
AKONDRO	NECTARINE
BERRY	VOASARY
SERIZY	PAPAY
VOANIO	PAISO
AVIL	POARA
VOALOP	MANANASY
GOAVY	RASPBERRY

59 - Engineering

```
G Z H P A Z O N X K L A S X
M E I N E J N I F W A X A A
I I A A N G O V O Z L I V N
M S L R A O F W B O I S A A
M D G I S H E R Y R N P I N
L A F F N A R E T O A M V E
D E G A N A R A Z I F T O R
I S V U W U W R T A G Y N O
E W Y E L A F I N Y L R Y N
S G J A R T I F A R S Y R A
E Y A N A S E F E R D N A F
L V K W M S A T U F I E S V
R A N O N J A V A T R A I W
W Y S B F I S F Y K S G K A
```

ZORO	ANGOVO
AXIS	INJENIE
KAJY	GEARS
FANORENANA	LEVERS
LALINA	RANON-JAVATRA
KISARY	MILINA
SAVAIVONY	FANDREFESANA
DIESEL	MAOTERA
LAFINY	HERY
FIZARANA	RAFITRA

60 - Government

```
K E G D O K O T I C B Z O M
J A I S A R K O M E D D G P
R U B F I T O V I A N A V I
U A H A K I R T S I D N C T
F K R C R Q X Y W F X J K A
S I E I H Y K I R A M J Y R
I T R J N Z L H A N O Q F I
V I L E A Y D N L J I A W K
I L Q A N A H A F A H A F A
L O D F À E V B T K E N R I
Y P F D L A N A R A S T I F
B P O T A B M A G N A S T I
R C M J L W V J T A P M F U
Z O M P I R E N E N A P N J
```

ZOM-PIRENENA   FAHAFAHANA
SIVILY   TSANGAMBATO
DEMOKRASIA   FIRENENA
DISTRIKA   POLITIKA
FITOVIANA   ZO
FITSARANA   KABARY
RARINY   FANJAKANA
LALÀNA   MARIKY
MPITARIKA

61 - Art Supplies

```
F A K A N T S A R Y G G M Q
P S O L I K A B J S U L F X
L E O A C R Y L I C U I G D
A A N M T E S E A M A H O L
K Z A S F E H S F N R C R L
A H R N I A T A R A T A S Y
O K O L M L M E X Z I R Q S
L A T Y C U I O E E V J A O
Y N I B S K N H R S E I T R
P A S T E L S C A O H G C O
S A R I B A O D A Z N L D B
R I E M G W A H A M O A G O
A G N A M I N A T T D H N A
U M T K E C G O V R V T H A
```

ACRYLIC
BOROSY
FAKANTSARY
SEZA
SARIBAO
TANIMANGA
LOKO
FAMORONANA
EASEL
GAOMA

LAKAOLY
HEVITRA
INK
SOLIKA
TARATASY
PASTELS
PENSILIHAZO
LOHA
RANO

62 - Science Fiction

```
I  A  R  T  A  O  H  A  F  A  T  F  D  M
S  R  G  N  O  F  I  N  O  F  Y  I  Y  I
J  A  M  E  T  Y  K  O  B  M  K  P  S  S
O  T  R  E  A  X  M  A  R  B  T  O  T  T
U  N  S  I  L  A  V  I  T  R  A  A  O  E
A  A  U  C  M  L  Z  J  H  P  N  H  P  R
U  T  E  L  C  A  R  O  R  L  M  A  I  Y
T  Z  O  X  A  G  H  L  B  A  F  N  A  H
O  F  F  M  M  E  R  O  Z  N  E  A  C  G
P  W  A  U  I  X  C  N  S  E  N  O  L  C
I  P  D  V  L  K  D  K  W  T  E  L  V  G
A  I  U  Z  U  D  A  E  K  A  Z  I  K  J
F  U  T  U  R  I  S  T  I  C  V  Y  G  V
Z  A  V  A  M  I  S  Y  S  W  S  R  A  N
```

ATOMIKA	GALAXY
BOKY	NOFINOFY
SARIMAHO	MISTERY
CLONES	TANTARA
LAVITRA	ORACLE
DYSTOPIA	PLANETA
FIPOAHANA	ZAVA-MISY
TAFAHOATRA	TEKNOLOJIA
AFO	UTOPIA
FUTURISTIC	

63 - Geometry

```
G T E L O Z O R O S A A U O
F A N A L O B I R A F R M E
L O G I C C R P V V P A A V
G F P Z P S T F C A J K R M
C A F A R I T R A I S A I T
M S Y M M E T R Y V A R N E
L I E I N V R O J O M A D O
M A T W U R A Y A N P K R R
E V M O G U I N K Y A A A I
D X G E V C M I R A H U N A
I U E P S Y R F P H A T O K
A S G O T A N A B S N D R L
N V A J T X N L A Y Y C O U
H A H A V O N Y V U C D Z P
```

ZORO	LAMESA
KAJY	MEDIAN
FARIBOLANA	ISA
CURVE	MITOVY
SAVAIVONY	ARAKARAKA
LAFINY	AMPAHANY
MIRA	FARITRA
HAHAVONY	SYMMETRY
MARINDRANO	TEORIA
LOGIC	TELOZORO

64 - Airplanes

```
B A L O N A O J Y Q H T K H
A L E F D R T P M I Y A G A
B L A O H A W W P I D R F H
A G T N T H K N A N R I A A
M D K I I G U M N J O D N V
B E G J T T W H A E G A O O
A P L J Z U R P M N È L R N
K N G I S E D A O I N A E Y
A F C Z P I K E R E E N N Z
N R I V O T R A Y P Z A A X
A S M P A N D E H A P S N I
R F I P E T R A H A N A A N
A T M O S F É R A S F V M Y
T U T A N T A R A F A P K Y
```

RIVOTRA	INJENIE
ALTITUDE	FEL
ATMOSFÉRA	HAHAVONY
BALONA	TANTARA
FANORENANA	HYDROGÈNE
EKIP	FIPETRAHANA
TARANAKA	MPANDEHA
DESIGN	MPANAMORY
TARI-DALANA	LANITRA

65 - Ocean

```
V V K G J D O S E F P M V X
X P G W F S Y A A R I S Q O
M J M H Q A S H G M C V H O
C O R A L M T I E Q O V X K
Y V A P H B E D E J A N Y S
F X D M O O R R L R N D T P
H O R I T A E A S S O T J A
L R Q R Q M L N W P Z U L Z
F D X H L U V O D U O O V O
A N T S A N T S A W R N G F
F O W V J P G C X T T B G M
L R D R I V O T R A H Z D E
R T J E L L Y F I S H O N B
W T U G S O K A T R A J N O
```

SAMBO	AHIDRANO
CORAL	ANTSANTSA
FOZA	SHRIMP
FESO	SPONGE
EEL	DRIVOTRA
TRONDRO	SAMONTA
JELLYFISH	THON
HORITA	SOKATRA
OYSTER	ONJA
SIRA	TROZONA

66 - Force and Gravity

```
F  M  S  I  T  E  N  G  A  M  L  N  F  N
W  B  T  N  O  S  C  S  A  C  A  D  O  A
F  I  Z  Ì  K  A  I  P  S  Y  N  F  T  H
C  E  N  T  R  E  M  N  Y  F  J  A  O  I
H  H  E  K  Z  T  A  H  D  E  A  N  A  T
X  A  A  D  F  M  N  H  C  R  U  I  N  A
S  N  I  I  Q  S  Y  V  L  D  Y  T  A  N
P  A  C  N  H  U  D  C  S  I  X  A  T  A
C  L  V  I  G  E  D  L  A  R  O  R  E  M
G  E  T  Q  N  O  T  H  H  A  B  A  N  W
N  N  I  B  Q  A  I  S  E  M  H  N  A  U
H  A  T  Z  A  R  B  P  I  B  Q  A  L  E
I  L  T  F  K  X  R  N  X  K  C  I  P  J
Y  E  U  H  J  H  O  K  V  G  A  D  L  X
```

AXIS	HAIHETSIKA
CENTRE	ORBIT
NAHITANA	FIZÌKA
ELANELANA	PLANETA
DYNAMIC	TSINDRY
FANITARANA	HAINGO
MAGNETISM	FOTOANA
MARIDREFY	LANJA

67 - Birds

```
H V W C F S D G L A N S A T
H L T U L T C Y Y A F A K O
K Z T C A O X D S O O M O U
F F B K M R S G A N A A H C
X O L O I K W X S A B L O A
E Y D O N R A C I V V O A N
F K H Y G A N R G G V B A S
D O V E O C A N A R Y M N A
G L A T O D Y D F C R O W D
V O R O N D R A N O D R Y M
E B A O T I R I S Y L O W I
V O R O M A H E R Y N V R H
B V W L G K X J S Y O J F Y
Q J U N Z J C M T Z H O X A
```

CANARY
AKOHO
CROW
CUCKOO
DOVE
GANA
VOROMAHERY
ATODY
FLAMINGO
GISA

VANO
AOTIRISY
BOLOKY
VOROMBOLA
SAMA
VORONDRANO
FODY
STORK
SWAN
TOUCAN

68 - Gymnastics

```
X V T T M H G Y M N A S T S
A N A S P L P J A J R N O O
X H N A A N A R A Z A H A F
K U A O N A H S E K I P A M
H A N K A L R D A E B M N T
X E A A Z T A R A S T I P M
M N R T A R B A E X V T S Z
T O B Y T E G T S R Z I N Q
T V Z R R A N O L O U G M A
R N F I A J Y E G G C W R T
H E K N K N L L G D Z G N S
O T L H O A N A Z I A H A F
O A N I K I B M A S T I M L
P A B M O K A B M O K I S T
```

FAHAIZANA
TSAOKA
MPANAZATRA
TSIKOMBAKOMBA
KIANJA
GYMNASTS
TANANA
HOOP

OLONA
MPITSARA
MITSAMBIKINA
LEOTARDS
MOZIKA
FAHAZARANA
HERY
EKIPA

69 - Nutrition

```
D A S G N D Z C O S I K Y W
I F R X L A A M A L A S S I
G I O T C L V S A K A F O K
E H A N A M A L A S A H A F
S I T I X V M Y D A X D S G
T N I X R R A N A M O K L L
I A L O Q K N J K F L V A I
O N A P Y D I G N A M Y N O
N A K Z K L T T D O T A J S
O D I I L I R K S K N P A I
G Z T E S L A K Y I O A Z D
V I T A M I N I N A R Q R A
F A H A Z A R A N A K O P Y
F E R M E N T A T I O N M E
```

KOMANA
MANGIDY
KALSET
GLIOSIDA
SAKAFO
DIGESTION
FIHINANA
FERMENTATION
TSIRO
FAHAZARANA

FAHASALAMANA
SALAMA
RANON-JAVATRA
KALITAO
SAOSY
ZAVA-MANITRA
POXIN
VITAMININA
LANJA

70 - Hiking

```
N S O L M T O E T R A I D T
K O X P O T A B M A R A H E
N F U L K J N K Y B I B Y U
O U A U A N A N A M O I F V
Z U J I D I N L R R M Y T Y
V A O N A R O O T Z E G O L
M H R E Z L V Z A P O R E O
G K D I O B O A S U Y C T T
K H N X D G V T E O E A R V
V X A S T A P O V M T V A A
C P O C S Q I M A F A L N T
D M S L F Q O N M O E P D O
D P A C I B W B A G K E R C
E B M K I R A R O M U L O W
```

BIBY
KIRARO
HARAMBATO
TOETRANDRO
LOZA
MAVESATRA
MAP
MOKA
TOETRA

ZARIDAINA
FIOMANANA
VATO
VOVONANA
MASOANDRO
RERAKA
RANO
DIA

71 - Professions #1

```
L Y M L M F E Y B C C T K A
C H Z B Q P I D W K J A I S
A I Y J V D A R S U J I M T
R D F O V O N A J I L A R
E N P S A F N Z A V A O V O
T A N T S A M B O Z A R L N
O P P X Y O V A Q A A K K O
K M Q L A N W D N N E T A M
O Z E R U O H U N T E R R A
D O X E M M A F M T B R T A
M O Z I K A B W X X M T H X
K M U Z M P R E G P C L U Z
J N C R A M Y Z R U U O F Z
M P H A R M A C I S T V Q Q
```

ASTRONOMA   FIRAVAKA
MPANAZATRA   MOZIKA
MPANDIHY   PHARMACIST
DOKOTERA   PLUMBER
MPAMONO AFO   TANTSAMBO
HUNTER   TAILOR

72 - Barbecues

```
M W C F P A S T V A O O L F
Q A T Y G Q A N A M A N A I
A Z F V R G O V A T A O V A
I N X A R I S X W O S H U N
K A T T N H Y Z O B L W I A
X N V S W A G E K A T O G K
A A L G Y E L I L P L Z R A
Y N G F I T R E B I K A I V
G A G X O A N K I Z Y K L I
M O Z I K A P N I I Y N L A
I N R Z K Z S Y D A L A S N
B A T O N G O L O O H O K A
Z H L E G I O M A Y U V C F
S A K A F O F W J X X X X T
```

AKOHO
ANKIZY
FIANAKAVIANA
SAKAFO
FITREBIKA
NAMANA
VOANKAZO
LALAO
GRILL
MAFANA

HANOANANA
ANTSY
MOZIKA
TONGOLO
SALADY
SIRA
SAOSY
VOATAVO
LEGIOMA

73 - Chocolate

```
I E T K G K M K W L C O V C
V O V O K A W A M Y Q F O V
L Y X A T S G W T A A J A A
C M A N G I D Y E S M X N T
D A Y E A O R I S T I Y I O
Y M C T N O D L L L S R O M
Y A K A Q A V K A N E G O A
W R T N O T N O K E E L J M
C I W A N I A L I L R E N Y
T S I R E L V D M R I U A N
B T L E M A R A C H B X O I
W Z J O I K O W U W A G V H
Y I M T N A D I X O I T N A
W X K D T U Q B U E E T S V
```

ANTIOXIDANT
MANGIDY
CACAO
KALSET
VATOMAMY
CARAMEL
VOANIO
MATSIRO
VAHINY

TOERANA TENA
ILAINA
VOANJO
VOVOKA
KALITAO
SIRAMAMY
MAMY
TSIRO

74 - Vegetables

```
T O N G O L O G A S Y Q Q K
S A K A M A L A H O D K I A
B A R A N J E L Y D A D L R
S F R V O A T A V O L W O A
P O V A M Y E P P I A G C O
Y Z F G N L B E C G S Z C T
K B R L F I H A K I R A O Y
R Ô I N E S P H O L A T R A
A B K R Q R P E F I A I B I
D O Q Ô P E A T O N G O L O
I G U C M P V O A T A B I A
S Q Z X W B T U R N I P V L
H S N F F Q R Q W R B C Q E
O L I V E Y M A I R E L E S
```

ARIKA
BROCCOLI
KARAOTY
SOFLERA
SELERIA
KÔKÔMBRA
BARANJELY
TONGOLO GASY
SAKAMALAHO
HOLATRA

OLIVE
TONGOLO
PERSILY
PEA
VOATAVO
RADISH
SALADY
EPINARA
VOATABIA
TURNIP

75 - The Media

```
N O M E R I K A O Z E R I J
S A M G A Z E T Y L X J N T
T N E M V P B G A A O R I O
F A N A B E A Z A N A N V R
O T I N E G A A Y R G B A I
N N L I K V R R E Z H A E N
W O N A R S T S I V D H V A
M N O S A L O C A L Z O A S
Z A D T D O R X K V X A W A
Q F Q A I E A Z J X A K M E
S J E R O S B Y M J B A W Q
D O K A M B A R O T R A Q F
F I F A N D R A I S A N A T
C X S W F S A R Y P L H A A
```

DOKAM-BAROTRA	ARA-TSAINA
ARA-BAROTRA	LOCAL
FIFANDRAISANA	REZO
NOMERIKA	GAZETY
FANONTANA	ONLINE
FANABEAZANA	SARY
OLONA	BAHOAKA
ORINASA	RADIO

76 - Boats

```
T E K I P Y A B A K A T M I
A G L R D O C K F A Q A A N
N O S A U U I W A Y N D S J
T N X N B E G R A M Y T E
S A K O O I K M I K W V E N
A R B M H W S O H B G S R I
M I X A R O Y A Y R A F T E
B N S S L Y G Y M E J D T E
O E D I T A A X H O B M A S
X R J N Q B K C D G N P J J
Z I E A O V N A H S L A T M
O S E A N A A W N T S T R I
U F F S P Y W S S A K C Q D
V A T O F A N T S I K A A X
```

VATOFANTSIKA   DRANOMASINA
BUOY   OSEANA
LAKANA   RAFT
EKIP   RENIRANO
DOCK   TADY
INJENIE   SAMBO
BAKA   TANTSAMBO
KAYAK   RANOMASINA
FARIHY   TIDE
MASTER   YACHT

77 - Driving

```
F M F M Q M K N G O G M W U
I U P F L Ô B A F O L D D L
T X H A E T S T M C F N B M
A U K M M Ô X G M I L Q Q Z
T B M A G I G C A K A T S C
E P A P F U L D B O Q O X K
R O O S A C L Y U G S C S I
A L T A N A L A D N A Y N E
N I E F A R E B N I L O Z A
A S R A Z F F Z D A D N G Y
C Y A B E N R Z E H L P A V
B U C C T F R E I N S A E N
W K R A E G A R A G S X L C
G N Y L T F I A R O V A N A
```

FREINS
TETEZANA
CAR
LOZA
MPAMILY
FEL
GARAGE
MAP
MAOTERA

MÔTÔ
POLISY
LALANA
FIAROVANA
HAINGO
ENY AN-DALANA
FITATERANA
KAMIAO

78 - Professions #2

```
M P A N A O G A Z E T Y E Z
X M B Y N E T Y N A B M O M
S A R Y Q V M R E M M Z T M
F I L O Z O F A S P P A R P
B U C M O H G S P A I R A A
Q E A O S A N A P M K I N N
R D N P A Y S K G P A D O D
F A A W B L K A W I R A M I
S G K F M O X P L A O I B D
B P D X H B F M M N K N O Y
M P A N A M O R Y A A A K Q
Q W P G Z A K P M T Y R Y G
M I M Y S P A J C R R X Y Y
H A S A I M I S Y A H A P M
```

MPANAMORY	TRANOMBOKY
MPIKAROKA	MOMBA NY TENY
MPAHAY SIMIA	MPANASOA
MPAMBOLY	FILOZOFA
ZARIDAINA	MPAKA SARY
SARY	MPANDIDY
MPANAO GAZETY	MPAMPIANATRA

79 - Mythology

```
A N D R I A M A N I T R A K
F I N O A N A X L D V I R O
C L I G R A M Z A J R B T L
T V P V M N A A B T S H I O
E X Y E K O H V Y L W M N N
L P J D H L E A R N O C A T
V Q Y L S A R B I Z Z Z L S
O M R T A I I O N A G N A A
G V E X E F F A T W E Y G I
S A H Y H H O R A N K L P N
M P I A D Y C Y I H I O W A
P R B E N V A R A T R A Q N
T S E L A T R A A B B Y O P
F I T O N D R A N T E N A V
```

ARCHETYPE
FITONDRANTENA
FINOANA
ZAVABOARY
KOLONTSAINA
ANDRIAMANITRA
LOZA
LANITRA

MAHERIFO
FIALONANA
LABYRINTA
ANGANO
TSELATRA
HERY
VARATRA
MPIADY

80 - Hair Types

```
I K T G D S C B Z O C W M M
W P Q R A K A F E L A M A A
M Q I E N T L L Y I J E T M
C A D Y I Y O A C O C Z E I
U P N M A Z S F N L F A V R
R L O I M F O H Y Y Y P I A
L S L R F Z N O I V S X N P
S F B B O Y D F L A T O A I
B J O O R G J M H W F C K R
E L A T O O M A I N T Y L A
Y D H W S G W S A L A M A T
V E M E D P N Q X L Y V R
M I R A N D R A N A R E R A
V O L A F O T S Y Y M X B W
```

SOLA	ELA
MAINTY	MAMIRAPIRATRA
BLOND	FOHY
MIRANDRANA	VOLAFOTSY
BROWN	MALEFAKA
CURL	MATEVINA
OLIOLY	MANIFY
MAINA	WAVY
GREY	FOTSY
SALAMA	

81 - Garden

```
A H I D R A T S Y I K U O T
P O Z A K N I N O V A H A A
V P Z R N F J Z M A R L I N
T M T T H K N U H E O W O I
S B V I R M V B V G H R W M
B E T H M A H A S A Y H J B
B N M A R R M V I R T S W A
H C B Z F P Z P J A U O O R
A H O Q A E M W O G H P B I
Z I Z F N B F Q N L O V U Z
O T A H O S E Y Z F I Y S A
Z O K B G W Y M F Y C N H H
K U A N I A D I R A Z A E D
D O B O M T E P E P P T X P
```

BENCH	SAHAM
BUSH	DOBO
FEFY	KAROHY
VONINKAZO	VATO
GARAGE	TANY
ZARIDAINA	TANIMBARIZA
AHITRA	TRAMPOLINE
HOSE	HAZO
BOZAKA	AHIDRATSY

82 - Countries #1

```
V M N W A I L A T I V Q V W
I O I P Y I X S U R F A U Z
E H K B B A M A N A P L T G
T B A N I A P S E K C E K R
N Z R O L E T O N J A M K J
A M A R S É N É G A L A C W
M Y G V E J I P T A R I H A
B D O E I S R A E L Y N E K
V R À Z F E E Y K W R A V O
Q J E Y A U V W K A N A D A
Q M D Z F I N L A N D E T R
Y A X A I N A M O R P Y O A
M P P V A L E O Z E N E V M
E B O D T S A N I N O L O P
```

BREZILA	MARAOKA
KANADA	NIKARAGOÀ
EJIPTA	NORVEZY
FINLANDE	PANAMA
ALEMAINA	POLONINA
IRAK	ROMANIA
ISRAELY	SÉNÉGAL
ITALIA	ESPAINA
LETONJA	VENEZOELA
LIBYA	VIETNAM

83 - Adjectives #1

```
T W E A N I R E D O A M T M
L S T A N T E R A K A A O I
Q B A N I Z I A M X S L N A
Z G A R T A B M A S M A G D
G A R T A S E V A M A L A A
S M V S D T B I C J T A L N
K J Y A Q G A A F B O T A A
K P F R D Z V R L M T A F M
X A I A E E D Y E B R N A A
W V N S P W H N I H A A T R
M D A T W F G I I P Y N R I
T O M T O B Y H B K D A A N
M A N I T R A A F E P X T A
D D T K Q C C V M I T O V Y
```

TANTERAKA	MARINA
MANITRA	BE
KANTO	MITOVY
TSARA TAREHY	ZAVA-DEHIBE
MAIZINA	MAODERINA
VAHINY	TONGA LAFATRA
MALALA-TANANA	MATOTRA
SAMBATRA	MIADANA
MAVESATRA	MANIFY
TSARA	

84 - Technology

```
I  F  H  R  H  W  X  O  V  P  E  U  N  A
A  N  O  R  D  N  O  T  I  K  V  W  O  N
Z  Y  T  X  J  M  Q  X  R  A  D  P  M  T
V  O  S  E  T  Y  B  O  T  C  A  T  E  O
B  L  O  G  R  D  K  K  O  R  A  Q  R  N
Y  R  A  S  T  N  A  K  A  F  S  S  I  T
V  I  L  W  W  D  E  C  L  R  O  E  K  A
H  A  F  A  T  R  A  T  Y  A  L  M  A  N
D  L  F  D  F  P  J  E  S  K  O  P  I  I
E  R  A  W  T  F  O  S  O  I  S  I  H  S
A  G  M  M  W  S  P  D  R  T  A  T  U  A
T  L  O  T  B  P  J  B  I  R  I  E  C  Q
C  C  C  O  M  A  F  L  V  A  N  T  U  A
F  I  K  A  R  O  H  A  N  A  A  Y  R  K
```

BLOG	HAFATRA
MPITETY	FIKAROHANA
BYTES	LAMBA
FAKANTSARY	ARO
SOLOSAINA	SOFTWARE
KITONDRO	ANTONTAN'ISA
NOMERIKA	VIRTOALY
RAKITRA	VIROSY
INTERNET	

85 - Landscapes

```
W H W U N R N H V R H L V E
N T O W J P F Z O A A O F F
W I N N W A Q L L N R H L I
O C B O A G L K K O A A A T
S K F U A H B I A M M S V R
E E C S Y S O N N A B A A A
A L T E S W I N O S A H B N
N G F C A E R S A I T A A A
A R E N I R A N O N O M T O
Q E E T U N D R A A C E O V
N B L S T O R A P A S I K A
L E V U Y H I R A F A U S H
G C F I E E G L A C I E R H
X I F I M O G B J D O Y T W
```

TORAPASIKA
LAVA-BATO
HARAMBATO
EFITRA
GEYSER
GLACIER
HAVOANA
ICEBERG
NOSY

FARIHY
OASIS
OSEANA
RENIRANO
RANOMASINA
HONAHONA
TUNDRA
LOHASAHA
VOLKANO

86 - Visual Arts

```
F H P E N S I L I H A Z O G
G A M J A T D P E N I N A G
T R M M P A N A K A N T O S
I T S O N A R T I R A M Y N
F I A Y R E J I F A B M O F
I K R O D O T S A O K A W P
F O Y I A G N A M I N A T O
E S F A S A N A G N A S G R
H Y R A S T N A N O R O H T
E R U N Z F H L L A U L T R
Z A K I M A R E S O G H V A
A S V R C C I S T X K Z B I
N S Q A G W X A X G H O M T
S T E N C I L E S A V O K A
```

NY MARITRANO
MPANAKANTO
SERAMIKA
TSAOKA
ARINA
TANIMANGA
FIFEHEZAN
FAMORONANA
EASEL
HORONAN-TSARY

SANGANASA
LOKO
PENINA
PENSILIHAZO
FOMBA FIJERY
SARY
PORTRAIT
SARY SOKITRA
STENCIL
SAVOKA

87 - Plants

```
R A V I N A Z A X S B S J V
C N U Y Z O A R L H E U Q O
B A B E A N R O O A R N Y N
W S E H Z W I L U K R K R I
N Y V I C I D F W M Y O I N
J N N T S N A H M L C Y N K
P E T A L S I A H I T R A A
U C R P T A N J S N B I M Z
L N W M F O A V U C D O A O
B Z P A J N B Z B U K F V K
F W R S S O M X B W T K A O
L A S Y I Z E Z I K A U Z D
O B K H A Z O B A M B O E E
O X J A M Q X F D L O Z M Q
```

BAMBO	ALA
BEAN	ZARIDAINA
BERRY	AHITRA
BOTANY	IVY
BUSH	MOSS
RAOZY	PETAL
ZEZIKA	FAKA
FLORA	SAMPA
VONINKAZO	HAZO
RAVINA	ZAVAMANIRY

88 - Boxing

```
P M B U M V Q Y R X T E R M
H Y D A T K X R Z K W D A I
F S C G F K W E O P F A T F
F O N O N T A N A N A K R A
T L M S I T R A N A R A A N
O O M P U I F H I P T Z M T
T K P H A N F S H C I V P O
O A I R E N R O C I V A I K
H L T P Y S O R E G E T A A
O W S J N N H H E P H A D B
N V A H J S I P I R T N Y U
D S R R E Z K T O T A A U B
R P A B N C Y I Y R R K L J
Y R E H D E I E A T L A A L
```

LAKOLOSY   FONON-TANANA
VATANA   RATRA
CHIN   DAKA
CORNER   MPANOHITRA
KIHO   HEVITRA
RERAKA   SITRANA
MPIADY   MPITSARA
TOTOHONDRY   TADY
MIFANTOKA   HERY

89 - Countries #2

```
S J D B F Q Y U R V L B L P
J A I L A M O S A M A X I A
C P A A N M U X E A O N B K
S O N P O X J J K R S I E I
I N I E N K I R R Z G Z R S
K N A N A D O S K N F E I T
R G R B B S D E W B C R A A
A U K A I S O R T L V I L N
M L O K L Y Y P Y I A A Y C
E G B A Y R Q H L N O R I G
N Z W A K I S K E M E P T K
A R A D N A G U O O P R I L
D R N X K I J A M A I K A A
R A H P M W A R F L E H H J
```

ALBANIA	MEKSIKA
DANEMARK	NEPAL
ETIOPIA	NIZERIA
GRESY	PAKISTAN
HAITI	ROSIA
JAMAIKA	SOMALIA
JAPON	SODANA
LAOS	SYRIA
LIBANONA	OUGANDA
LIBERIA	OKRAINA

90 - Adjectives #2

```
B F M A H A L I A N A N E N
Y R A H A N A J A O V O N A
J F F M M A L A Z A T A F N
D U Z B O A V O A V Y N A A
E G B A O R M U E Y F A M M
M A F A N A O A F L Y K A B
D R T G H P P N I G C A R O
M T E P C S Z I A N C N I N
S A H J A B R R G N A T T Y
A K A Q Y T S A M P A O A Q
L O T K P J J M L A Z F N R
A M O L I L U A Z G F R A D
M A R M A S I R A V H Y T I
A M Y A R A D A L À N A K A
```

MARINA	VOAJANAHARY
FAMORONANA	VAOVAO
FAMARITANA	ARA-DALÀNA
MAINA	MAMOKATRA
KANTO	NANAMBONY
MALAZA	MASIRA
SALAMA	TE HATORY
MAFANA	MAFY
NOANA	DIA
MAHALIANA	

91 - Psychology

```
F O P M A H E S T E H I F F
F I L C O G N I T I O N F I
A N T A N A O B A S T I P T
H J S S N F I T A O M A N O
A T H D A A R T I V E H S N
Z T K O O B X K T V I O P D
A R T E O T O H O R D O I R
Z E K Y S I M A V A Z O Z A
A N A N A B M O N A F U P N
N Z Y B Y K F D J A H D P T
A K F I F A N D I R A N A E
L P O F A N E N D R E N A N
A Y N I N A H O N N I D O A
G R W F O M B A F I J E R Y
```

FANENDRENA
FANOMBANANA
FITONDRANTENA
FAHAZAZANA
PITSABOANA
COGNITION
FIFANDIRANA
NOFY
HEVITRA

FITAOMAN
FOMBA FIJERY
TOETRA
OLANA
ZAVA-MISY
FIHETSEHAM-PO
NOHANINY
FITSABOANA

92 - Math

```
I S Y M M E T R Y A M P R P
Y S H G W J O Y I M A A A E
D Q A C F J E F O P H R F R
Y N O V I A V A S A I I I P
N R L Q F O Q L E H T T T E
M Y A Z J Z B O L A S R R N
X Z D S K X O R B N I A I D
N V V I T R K A A Y S C S I
V O L A V I Y M A G J R A C
C I R C U M F E R E N C E U
M M I T O V Y A L V X X X L
V I B D Q U T A R D X H N A
M A R G O L E L L A R A P R
V H H A T E L O Z O R O Z C
```

RAFITRISA
CIRCUMFERENCE
SAVAIVONY
MIRA
AMPAHANY
RAFITSARY
ISA
MITOVY
PARALLELOGRAM

PARITRA
PERPENDICULAR
MAROLAFY
MAHITSI-
VOLA
SYMMETRY
TELOZORO
BOKY

93 - Water

```
D S D K O N A R I N E R W M
A N O D C O F A N A L A K A
R E S Y E G E A A R I Y H N
O I B B A N A R O Y N L A D
N P V U N Y L U L U U Q T O
J I G O A D P A N O T E O F
A C C J D O U K L M C Z N A
O N A R D O F A S A I L D R
R R E A K R Z H I B N J R I
T T A N V O Q A J R Y A A H
O Y H N L A S A E T O N A Y
S K V J A L A N A P M A R O
I F A N D R O A N A U N E E
M Z H A M A N D O A N A G M
```

LALANA
MANDO
MISOTRO
LASA ETONA
SAFODRANO
FANALA
GEYSER
HATONDRA
RIVO-DOZA
FARIHY

HAMANDOANA
ORANA
OCEAN
NY ORANA
RENIRANO
FANDROANA
ORAM-PANALA
ETONA
ONJA

94 - Activities

```
Z  H  I  D  O  U  K  N  S  F  H  G  E  D
Z  A  Y  H  I  D  A  A  E  A  A  T  C  J
D  C  R  C  G  R  N  R  R  N  Z  M  N  V
A  S  A  I  I  R  T  T  A  J  A  O  Q  F
F  S  S  W  D  J  O  I  M  O  A  L  A  L
D  I  A  C  E  A  C  A  I  N  Z  Z  M  E
N  A  A  T  W  G  I  J  K  O  L  R  A  O
X  H  P  L  A  H  Q  N  A  A  M  Y  H  R
M  V  O  T  A  N  D  A  A  N  R  S  A  U
Z  T  D  L  B  M  A  M  Z  A  D  F  L  E
X  M  D  C  B  J  B  N  Y  R  E  T  I  P
C  H  J  B  N  M  J  O  A  T  R  I  A  R
K  N  I  T  T  I  N  G  L  O  D  Y  N  W
K  Y  K  I  G  L  X  I  A  Y  R  K  A  S
```

ASA	HAZA
KANTO	MAHALIANA
SERAMIKA	KNITTING
ASA-TANANA	FIALAM-BOLY
DIHY	ODY
FANJONOANA	SARY
LALAO	MANJAITRA
ZARIDAINA	

95 - Business

```
O  A  R  I  B  G  E  X  P  L  O  A  Q  F
M  R  B  A  A  D  H  N  F  E  L  A  S  H
P  T  I  U  I  E  O  W  R  H  L  R  X  P
A  O  M  N  C  V  N  S  K  I  V  T  F  S
M  R  H  I  A  L  T  Q  D  B  W  E  I  D
P  A  P  O  H  S  E  W  R  E  Y  H  D  F
I  B  Y  T  F  R  A  V  Y  N  I  D  I  V
A  M  Z  Z  E  N  S  G  I  Y  C  O  R  F
S  A  Y  H  L  T  A  W  W  T  T  R  A  Y
A  T  R  O  P  M  I  Y  Z  B  R  M  M  T
A  N  Y  E  F  N  P  B  I  P  Z  A  B  V
V  E  L  O  P  M  M  S  O  R  E  W  O  O
N  H  E  F  K  C  M  W  H  L  Z  R  L  L
N  Y  O  R  I  N  A  S  A  S  A  C  A  A
```

LEHIBENY	IMPORT
TETIBOLA	FIDIRAM-BOLA
ASA	ENTAM-BAROTRA
ORINASA	VOLA
VIDINY	BIRAO
LEVITRA	SALE
MPIASA	SHOP
MPAMPIASA	HETRA
NY ORINASA	

96 - Literature

```
M F A D T A N T A R A L M R
P A N E G H S E L F R N P H
A N A S L E H E O X T N I Y
N A L C Y T N U Z K I O T M
O K O R N D G R A R V F A E
R I G I Q P V F E M E O N M
A A Y P R H Y T H M K H T E
T N Z T X F T H E R O E A T
R A M I P S O A H C T Z R A
A N U O R V M M K L O I A F
E A J N H R O L B I F N S I
T O N O N K A L O A L A X R
F A M P I T A H A N A A M A
F A N A D I H A D I A N A P
```

ANALOGY
FANADIHADIANA
MPANORATRA
FAMPITAHANA
FANAKIANANA
DESCRIPTION
TAKILA
NOFOHEZINA
GENRE

METAFIRA
MPITANTARA
TANTARA
TONONKALO
RHYME
RHYTHM
FOMBA
FOTO-KEVITRA
LOZA

97 - Geography

```
T  T  W  I  R  A  N  O  M  A  S  I  N  A
Y  A  D  Z  S  S  J  E  Q  L  Y  L  A  S
N  W  N  W  F  A  R  T  I  R  A  F  T  I
L  O  I  À  E  L  M  K  G  M  C  J  S  R
A  B  S  L  N  T  W  P  N  E  Y  K  I  E
I  Y  M  Y  S  A  V  W  O  B  Z  Y  M  N
E  K  O  A  T  E  R  A  E  N  J  M  O  I
F  I  R  E  N  E  N  A  D  Q  I  O  V  R
L  O  R  M  A  P  N  M  U  O  P  N  P  A
F  A  R  I  T  A  N  Y  T  Z  L  Y  A  N
O  N  X  H  R  M  E  R  I  D  I  A  N  O
J  Q  A  P  L  A  T  I  T  U  D  E  V  C
A  V  A  R  A  T  R  A  L  B  D  H  L  O
F  R  Y  A  U  Q  M  Z  A  N  A  E  S  O
```

ALTITUDE	MERIDIAN
ATLAS	AVARATRA
TANÀNA	OSEANA
FIRENENA	FARITRA
ISAM-PONINA	RENIRANO
EKOATERA	RANOMASINA
NOSY	ATSIMO
LATITUDE	FARITANY
MAP	

98 - Jazz

```
A R I H K Y M H T Y H R G T
B M Y S I R O V A F J A E A
M V P Y W T Z E X K H K N L
O M A O L Q I D I T Z I R O
F A T O N A K A H E T K E H
J L B A V G A B H B A I I A
T A M Q L A A N M O B R T R
H Z N U A E O K I K E A X K
Q A A R I K N O R O M A P M
T E K N I K A T F A P M I T
I S A N A S I F A M A N A F
T O R K E S I T R A X P O Y
F A M P I S E H O A N A C R
F A N A M B A R A N A X S W
```

RAKIKIRA
TEHAKA
MPAMORON-KIRA
FAMPISEHOANA
AMPONGA
FANAMAFISANA
MALAZA
FAVORIS
GENRE
FANAMBARANA

MOZIKA
VAOVAO
TALOHA
ORKESITRA
RHYTHM
HIRA
FOMBA
TALENTA
TEKNIKA

99 - Nature

```
Y X N T J N O Z Z R W K R R
T Z L H A R E A A E R Y A A
N O Y D W J M V V N B H H V
J B N R U G O O A I I E O I
I U P Y C E F N D R B R N N
G L A C I E R A E A Y A A A
R A R Z I S C I H N L T V Z
I Q T W A M Z D I O E A A L
A U I S F C A N B I T R L S
K W F M X T G N E Y N A B A
A P E A B D U I Y K A S H E
A C T I C J E J T D T T C S
T A N Y M A F A N A J A M X
F I A L O F A N A B Y H W O
```

BIBY	RAVINA
ACTIC	ALA
HATSARATAREHY	GLACIER
TANTELY	RENIRANO
RAHONA	TONY
EFITRA	FIALOFANA
DYNAMIC	TANY MAFANA
RIAKA	ZAVA-DEHIBE
ZAVONA	DIA

100 - Electricity

```
Y I Z H U S Q F B Z L Z T D
B Y P O R G Z I C A K A E F
A B T S A R A T A A X V L I
L M Z T B W N A B Q A A E T
B A D N O T I O L E G T V E
A I S C E M N V E J B R I H
T R N E O B O A R W J A Z I
E D J B R W A N U E V J I R
R N Q G I K F A R I Z A O I
I A L S J Z E V D A Q O N Z
A Y T O S D L H O F T W I A
M D L K X I E S K L T S C N
R N L V L K T E K C O S Y A
H E R I N A R A T R A K L O
```

BATERIA	REZO
CABLE	ZAVATRA
HERINARATRA	TSARA
FITAOVANA	BE
GROPY	SOCKET
JIRO	FITEHIRIZANA
LASER	TELEFAONINA
ANDRIAMBY	TELEVIZION
RATSY	

1 - Antiques

2 - Food #1

3 - Measurements

4 - Farm #2

5 - Books

6 - Meditation

7 - Days and Months

8 - Energy

9 - Archeology

10 - Food #2

11 - Chemistry

12 - Music

13 - Family

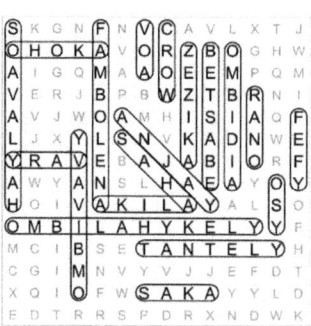

14 - Farm #1

15 - Camping

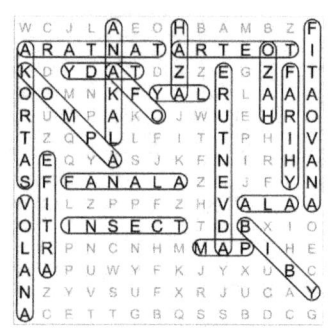

16 - Cats

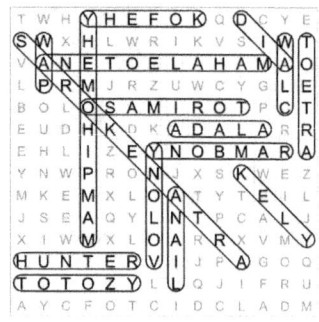

17 - Algebra

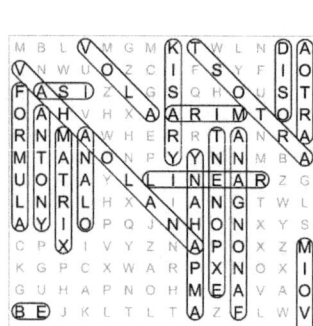

18 - Spices

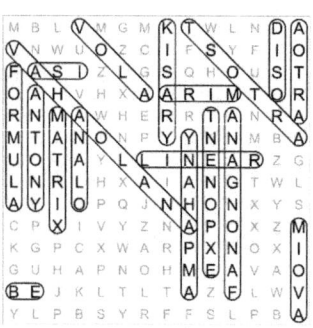

19 - Universe

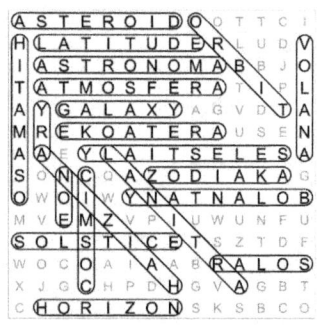

20 - Mammals

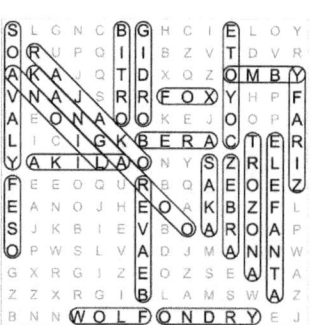

21 - Fishing

22 - Restaurant #1

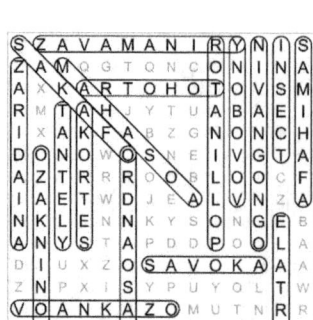

23 - Bees

24 - Photography

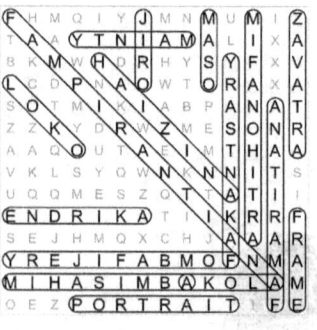

25 - Weather

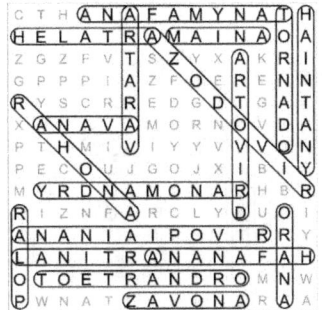

26 - Adventure

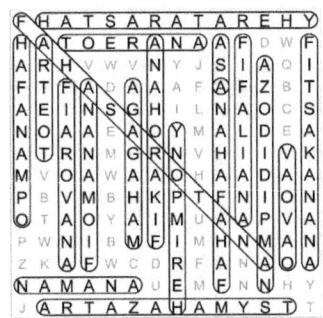

27 - Circus

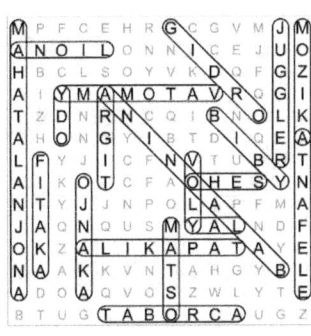

28 - Tools

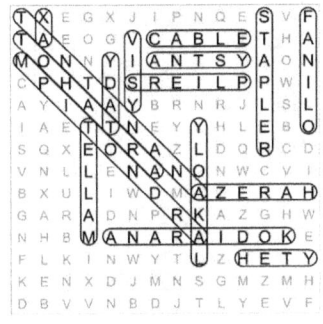

29 - Restaurant #2

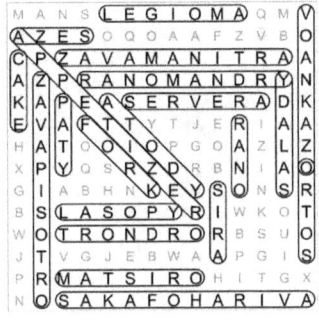

30 - Geology

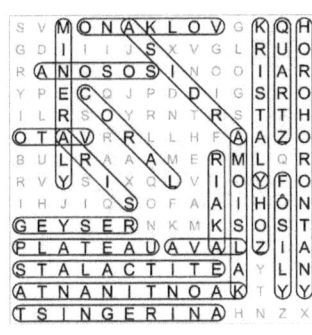

31 - House

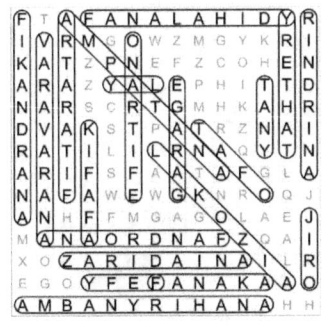

32 - Physics

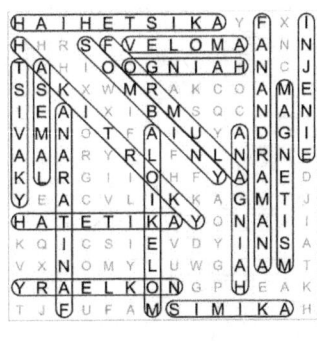

33 - Dance

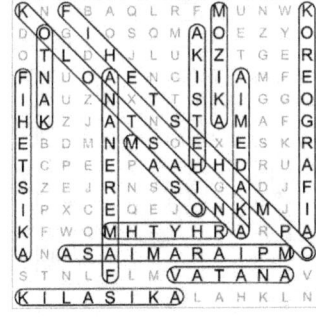

34 - Coffee

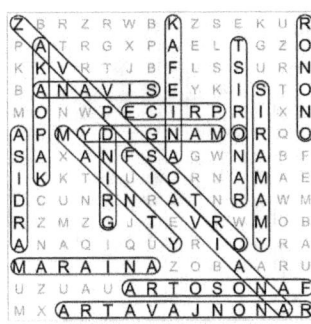

35 - Colors

36 - Shapes

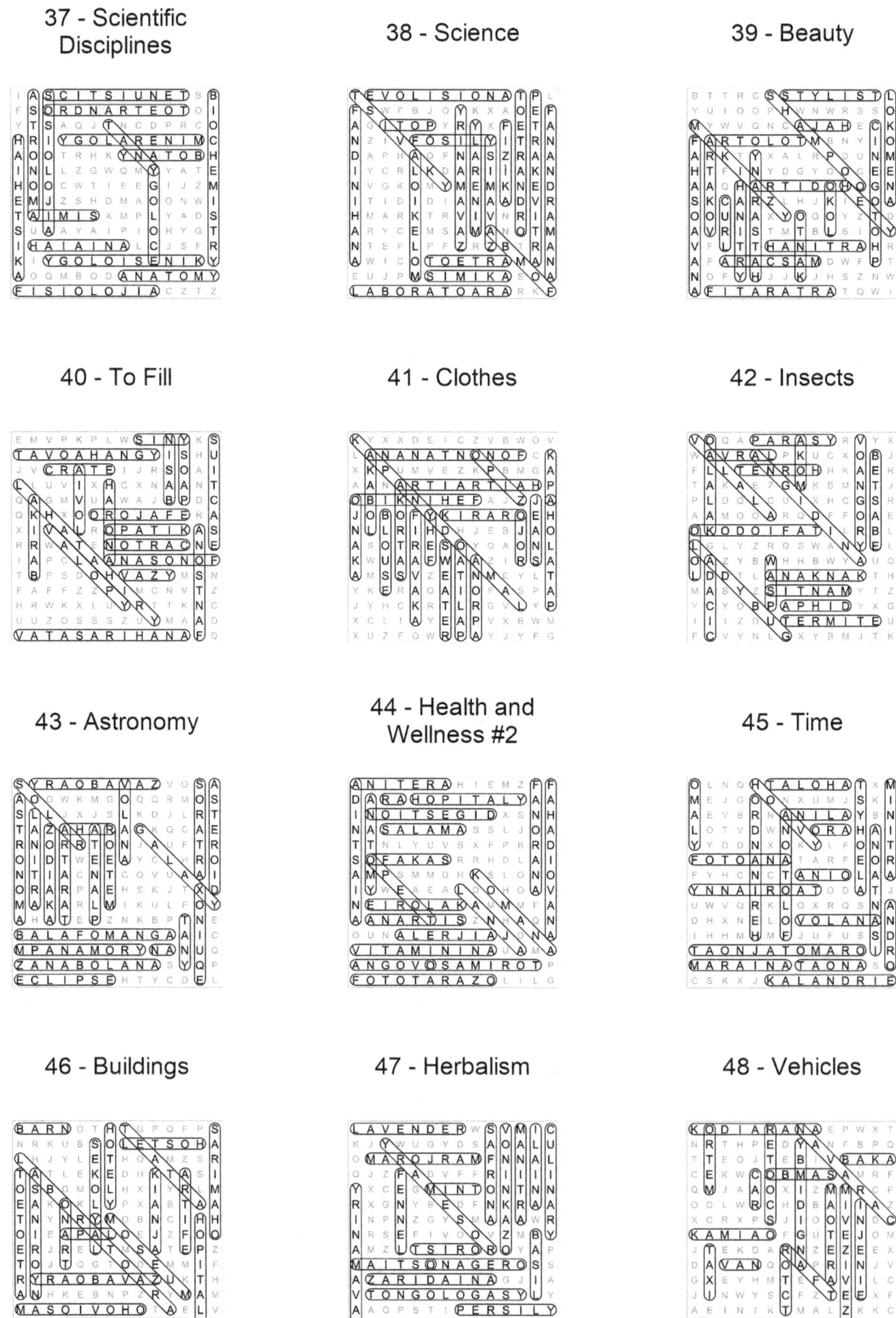

37 - Scientific Disciplines

38 - Science

39 - Beauty

40 - To Fill

41 - Clothes

42 - Insects

43 - Astronomy

44 - Health and Wellness #2

45 - Time

46 - Buildings

47 - Herbalism

48 - Vehicles

49 - Flowers

50 - Health and Wellness #1

51 - Town

52 - Antarctica

53 - Ballet

54 - Fashion

55 - Human Body

56 - Musical Instruments

57 - Cooking Tools

58 - Fruit

59 - Engineering

60 - Government

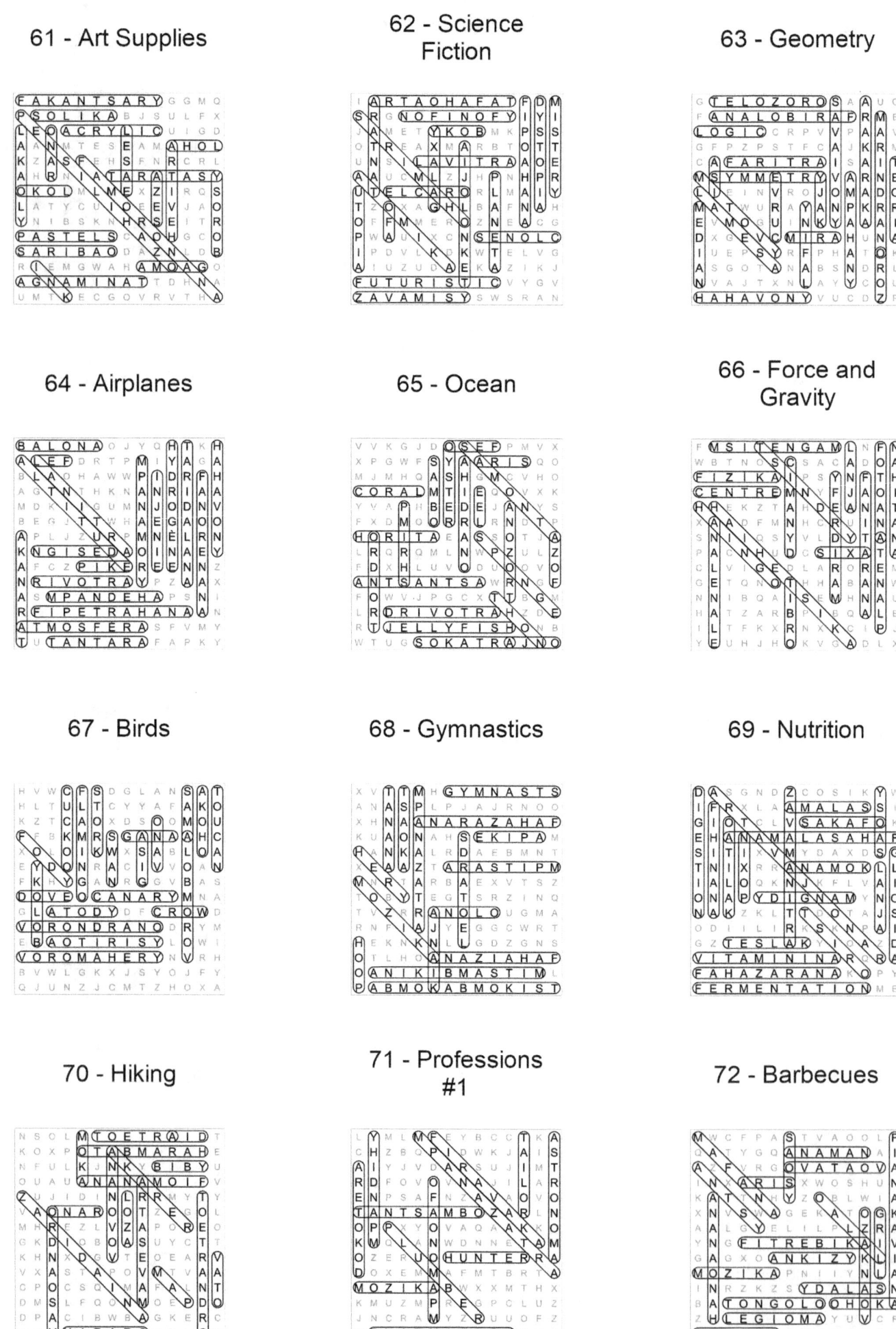

61 - Art Supplies

62 - Science Fiction

63 - Geometry

64 - Airplanes

65 - Ocean

66 - Force and Gravity

67 - Birds

68 - Gymnastics

69 - Nutrition

70 - Hiking

71 - Professions #1

72 - Barbecues

73 - Chocolate

74 - Vegetables

75 - The Media

76 - Boats

77 - Driving

78 - Professions #2

79 - Mythology

80 - Hair Types

81 - Garden

82 - Countries #1

83 - Adjectives #1

84 - Technology

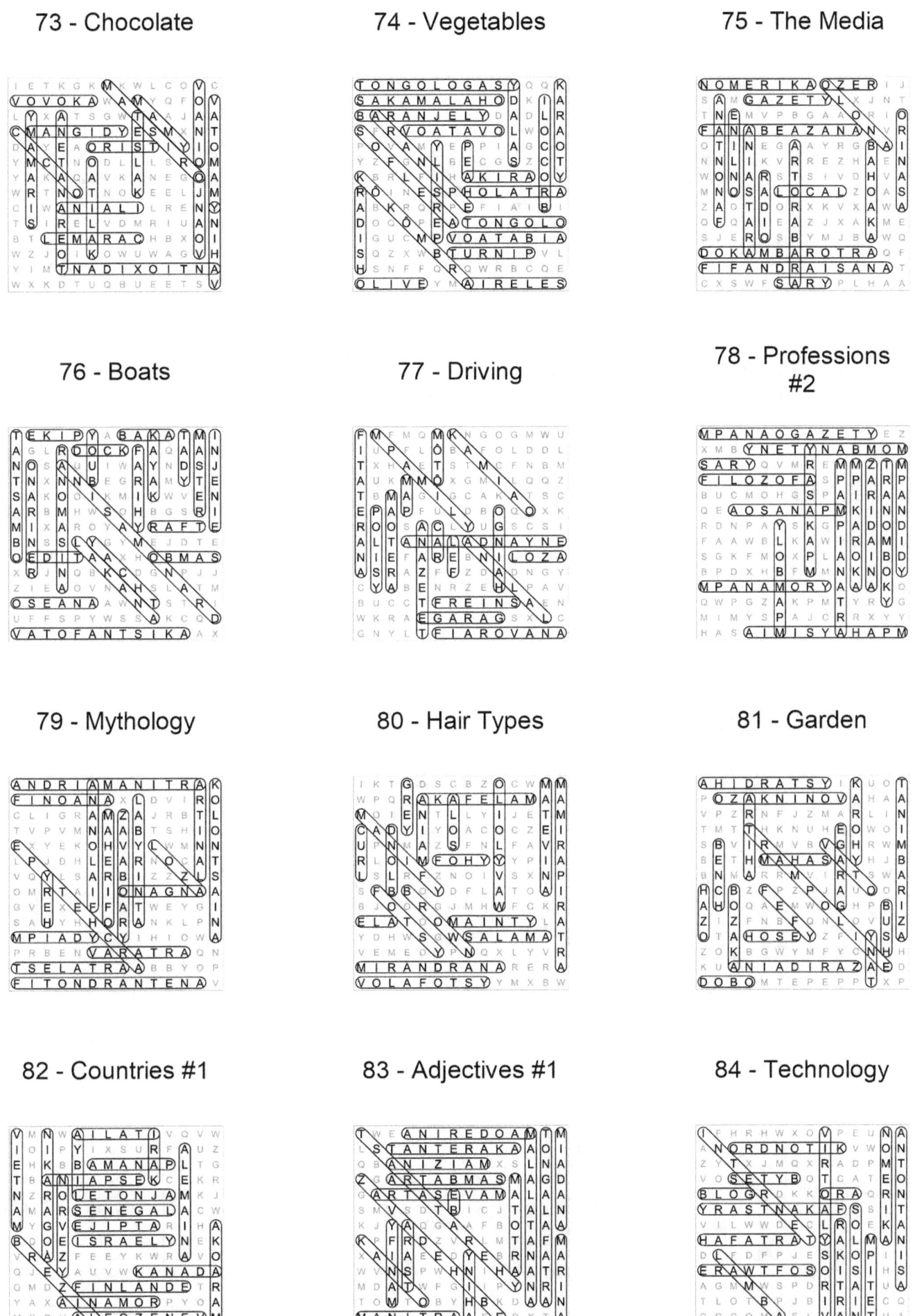

85 - Landscapes

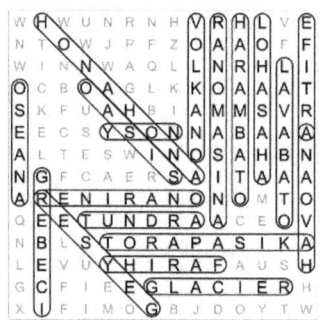

86 - Visual Arts

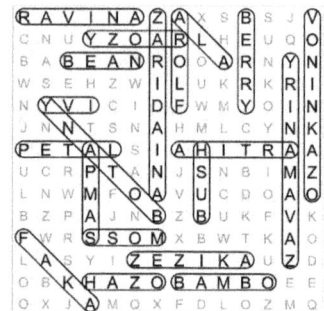

87 - Plants

88 - Boxing

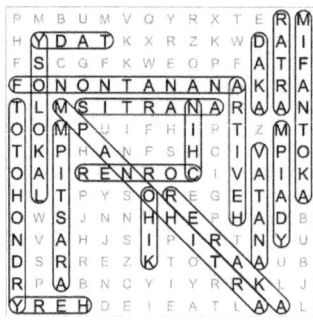

89 - Countries #2

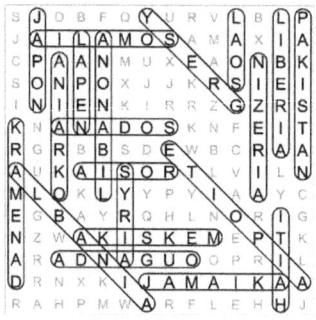

90 - Adjectives #2

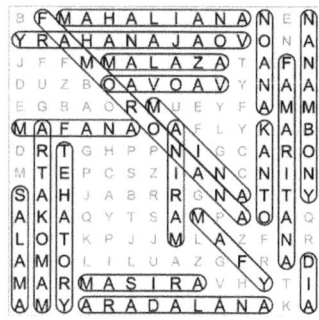

91 - Psychology

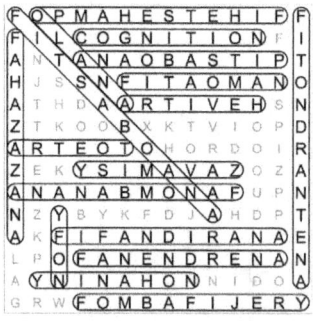

92 - Math

93 - Water

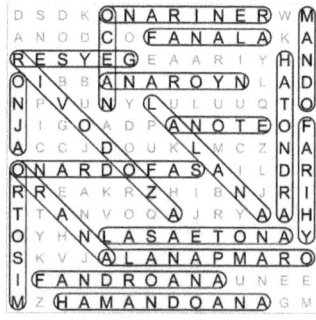

94 - Activities

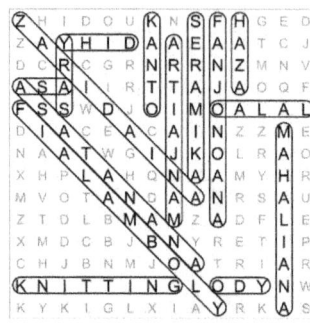

95 - Business

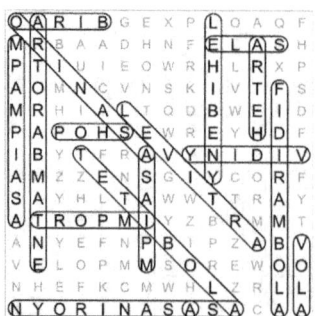

96 - Literature

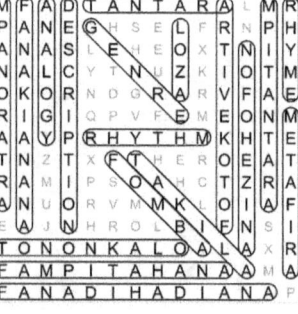

97 - Geography

98 - Jazz

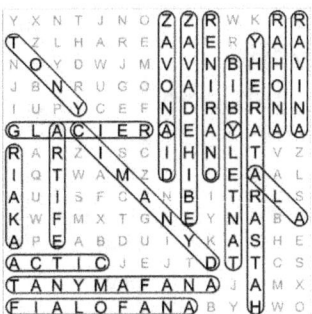

99 - Nature

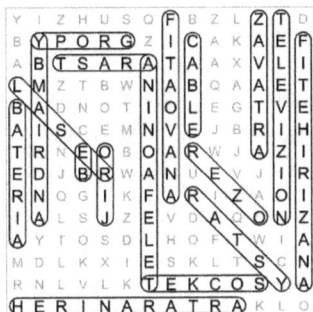

100 - Electricity

Dictionary

Activities
Fiaraha-Mientana

Activity	Asa
Art	Kanto
Ceramics	Seramika
Crafts	Asa-Tanana
Dancing	Dihy
Fishing	Fanjonoana
Games	Lalao
Gardening	Zaridaina
Hunting	Haza
Interests	Mahaliana
Knitting	Knitting
Leisure	Fialam-Boly
Magic	Ody
Photography	Sary
Sewing	Manjaitra

Adjectives #1
Adjektiva #1

Absolute	Tanteraka
Aromatic	Manitra
Artistic	Kanto
Attractive	Tsara Tarehy
Dark	Maizina
Exotic	Vahiny
Generous	Malala-Tanana
Happy	Sambatra
Heavy	Mavesatra
Helpful	Tsara
Honest	Marina
Huge	Be
Identical	Mitovy
Important	Zava-Dehibe
Modern	Maoderina
Perfect	Tonga Lafatra
Serious	Matotra
Slow	Miadana
Thin	Manify
Valuable	Sarobidy

Adjectives #2
Adjektiva #2

Authentic	Marina
Creative	Famoronana
Descriptive	Famaritana
Dry	Maina
Elegant	Kanto
Famous	Malaza
Gifted	Manan-Talenta
Healthy	Salama
Hot	Mafana
Hungry	Noana
Interesting	Mahaliana
Natural	Voajanahary
New	Vaovao
Normal	Ara-Dalàna
Productive	Mamokatra
Proud	Nanambony
Salty	Masira
Sleepy	Te Hatory
Strong	Mafy
Wild	Dia

Adventure
Traikefa Nahafinaritra

Activity	Asa
Beauty	Hatsaratarehy
Bravery	Herim-Pony
Dangerous	Nampidi-Doza
Destination	Toerana
Difficulty	Fahasarotana
Enthusiasm	Hafanam-Po
Excursion	Fitsakanana
Friends	Namana
Joy	Fifaliana
Nature	Toetra
Navigation	Fikarohana
New	Vaovao
Opportunity	Fahafahana
Preparation	Fiomanana
Safety	Fiarovana
Surprising	Mahagaga
Unusual	Tsy Mahazatra

Airplanes
Fiaramanidina

Adventure	Adventure
Air	Rivotra
Altitude	Altitude
Atmosphere	Atmosféra
Balloon	Balona
Construction	Fanorenana
Crew	Ekip
Descent	Taranaka
Design	Design
Direction	Tari-Dalana
Engine	Injenie
Fuel	Fel
Height	Hahavony
History	Tantara
Hydrogen	Hydrogène
Landing	Fipetrahana
Passenger	Mpandeha
Pilot	Mpanamory
Sky	Lanitra
Turbulence	Misafotofoto

Algebra
Alijebra

Diagram	Kisary
Equation	Mira
Exponent	Exponent
Factor	Antony
False	Diso
Formula	Formula
Fraction	Ampahany
Linear	Linear
Matrix	Matrix
Number	Isa
Problem	Olana
Quantity	Be
Simplify	Tsotra
Solution	Vahaolana
Subtraction	Fanongana
Sum	Vola
Variable	Miova
Zero	Aotra

Antarctica
Any Amin'ny Tendrontany

Bay	Bay
Birds	Vorona
Clouds	Rahona
Continent	Kaontinanta
Cove	Cove
Expedition	Dia
Exploration	Fitrandrahana
Geography	Jeografia
Ice	Ranomandry
Islands	Nosy
Minerals	Mineraly
Peninsula	Saikinosy
Researcher	Mpikaroka
Rocky	Vatolampy
Scientific	Siantifika
Temperature	Hafanana
Topography	Topography
Water	Rano
Whales	Trozona
Winds	Rivotra

Antiques
Rakitry ny Ela

Auction	Lavanty
Authentic	Marina
Century	Taonjato Maro
Coins	Vola Madinika
Collector	Hetra
Condition	Toe-Javatra
Decorative	Haingon-Trano
Elegant	Kanto
Furniture	Fanaka
Gallery	Gallery
Item	Zavatra
Jewelry	Firavaka
Old	Taloha
Price	Price
Quality	Kalitao
Sculpture	Sary Sokitra
Style	Fomba
Unusual	Tsy Mahazatra
Value	Sarobidy

Archeology
Arkeolojia

Analysis	Fanadihadiana
Ancient	Fahiny
Bones	Taolana
Civilization	Sivilizasiona
Era	Era
Evaluation	Tombana
Fossil	Fôsily
Mystery	Zava-Miafina
Objects	Zavatra
Professor	Profesora
Relic	Vakoka
Researcher	Mpikaroka
Team	Ekipa
Temple	Tempoly
Tomb	Fasana
Unknown	Tsy Fantatra
Years	Taona

Art Supplies
Fitaovana Zavakanto

Acrylic	Acrylic
Brushes	Borosy
Camera	Fakantsary
Chair	Seza
Charcoal	Saribao
Clay	Tanimanga
Colors	Loko
Creativity	Famoronana
Easel	Easel
Eraser	Gaoma
Glue	Lakaoly
Ideas	Hevitra
Ink	Ink
Oil	Solika
Paper	Taratasy
Pastels	Pastels
Pencils	Pensilihazo
Table	Loha
Water	Rano

Astronomy
Ny Vintana

Asteroid	Asteroid
Astronaut	Mpanamory
Astronomer	Astronoma
Constellation	Soratra
Earth	Tany
Eclipse	Eclipse
Equinox	Equinox
Galaxy	Galaxy
Meteor	Meteor
Moon	Volana
Nebula	Na
Observatory	Zavaboary
Planet	Planeta
Radiation	Taratra
Rocket	Balafomanga
Satellite	Zanabolana
Sky	Lanitra
Solar	Solar
Supernova	Raha
Zodiac	Zodiaka

Ballet
Resaka Teatra, Dihy

Applause	Tehaka
Artistic	Kanto
Audience	Mpihaino
Ballerina	Ballerina
Choreography	Koreografia
Composer	Mpamoron-Kira
Dancers	Mpandihy
Gesture	Fihetsika
Intensity	Mafy
Lessons	Lesona
Muscles	Hozatra
Music	Mozika
Orchestra	Orkesitra
Rehearsal	Famerenana
Rhythm	Rhythm
Solo	Solo
Style	Fomba
Technique	Teknika

Barbecues
Barbecues

Chicken	Akoho
Children	Ankizy
Dinner	Sakafo Hariva
Family	Fianakaviana
Food	Sakafo
Forks	Fitrebika
Friends	Namana
Fruit	Voankazo
Games	Lalao
Grill	Grill
Hot	Mafana
Hunger	Hanoanana
Knives	Antsy
Music	Mozika
Onions	Tongolo
Salads	Salady
Salt	Sira
Sauce	Saosy
Tomatoes	Voatavo
Vegetables	Legioma

Beauty
Hatsaran-Tarehy

Charm	Hatsarany
Color	Loko
Cosmetics	Makiazy
Curls	Curl
Elegance	Haja
Elegant	Kanto
Fragrance	Hanitra
Grace	Fahasoavana
Lipstick	Lokomena
Mascara	Mascara
Mirror	Fitaratra
Photogenic	Photogenic
Products	Vokatra
Scent	Hanitry
Scissors	Hety
Services	Tolotra
Shampoo	Shampoo
Skin	Hoditra
Stylist	Stylist

Bees
Tantely

Beneficial	Mahasoa
Diversity	Samihafa
Flowers	Voninkazo
Food	Sakafo
Fruit	Voankazo
Garden	Zaridaina
Hive	Tohotra
Honey	Tantely
Insect	Insect
Plants	Zavamaniry
Pollen	Vovobony
Pollinator	Pollinator
Queen	Mpanjakavavy
Smoke	Setroka
Sun	Masoandro
Swarm	Nivangongo
Wax	Savoka
Wings	Elatra

Birds
Vorona

Canary	Canary
Chicken	Akoho
Crow	Crow
Cuckoo	Cuckoo
Dove	Dove
Duck	Gana
Eagle	Voromahery
Egg	Atody
Flamingo	Flamingo
Goose	Gisa
Heron	Vano
Ostrich	Aotirisy
Parrot	Boloky
Peacock	Vorombola
Pelican	Sama
Penguin	Vorondrano
Sparrow	Fody
Stork	Stork
Swan	Swan
Toucan	Toucan

Boats
Sambo

Anchor	Vatofantsika
Buoy	Buoy
Canoe	Lakana
Crew	Ekip
Dock	Dock
Engine	Injenie
Ferry	Baka
Kayak	Kayak
Lake	Farihy
Mast	Master
Nautical	Dranomasina
Ocean	Oseana
Raft	Raft
River	Renirano
Rope	Tady
Sailboat	Sambo
Sailor	Tantsambo
Sea	Ranomasina
Tide	Tide
Yacht	Yacht

Books
Boky

Adventure	Adventure
Author	Mpanoratra
Character	Toetra
Collection	Famoriam-Bola
Context	Manodidina
Duality	Duality
Epic	Epic
Historical	Ara-Tantara
Humorous	Vazivazy
Immersion	Asitrika
Inventive	Mamorona
Literary	Haisoratra
Narrator	Mpitantara
Novel	Tantara
Page	Pejy
Poem	Tononkalo
Reader	Mpamaky
Relevant	Manan-Danja
Tragic	Nijaly
Words	Teny

Boxing
Ady Totohondry

Bell	Lakolosy
Body	Vatana
Chin	Chin
Corner	Corner
Elbow	Kiho
Exhausted	Reraka
Fighter	Mpiady
Fist	Totohondry
Focus	Mifantoka
Gloves	Fonon-Tanana
Injuries	Ratra
Kick	Daka
Opponent	Mpanohitra
Points	Hevitra
Recovery	Sitrana
Referee	Mpitsara
Ropes	Tady
Strength	Hery

Buildings
Tranobe

Apartment	Trano
Barn	Barn
Cabin	Efitra
Castle	Lapa
Cinema	Sarimaho
Embassy	Masoivoho
Factory	Ny Orinasa
Hospital	Hopitaly
Hostel	Hostel
Hotel	Hotely
Laboratory	Laboratoara
Museum	Moseum
Observatory	Zavaboary
School	Sekoly
Stadium	Kianja
Supermarket	Toetoetra
Tent	Lay
Theater	Teatra
Tower	Tilikambo
University	Oniversite

Business
Raharaham-Barotra

Boss	Lehibeny
Budget	Tetibola
Career	Asa
Company	Orinasa
Cost	Vidiny
Discount	Levitra
Employee	Mpiasa
Employer	Mpampiasa
Factory	Ny Orinasa
Import	Import
Income	Fidiram-Bola
Merchandise	Entam-Barotra
Money	Vola
Office	Birao
Sale	Sale
Shop	Shop
Taxes	Hetra

Camping
Filasiana

Adventure	Adventure
Animals	Biby
Cabin	Efitra
Canoe	Lakana
Compass	Kompà
Equipment	Fitaovana
Fire	Afo
Forest	Ala
Hat	Satroka
Hunting	Haza
Insect	Insect
Lake	Farihy
Lantern	Fanala
Map	Map
Moon	Volana
Nature	Toetra
Rope	Tady
Stories	Tantara
Tent	Lay
Trees	Hazo

Cats
Ny Saka

Claw	Claw
Crazy	Adala
Curious	Liana
Funny	Mampihomehy
Fur	Volony
Hunter	Hunter
Independent	Mahaleotena
Little	Kely
Mouse	Totozy
Paw	Paw
Personality	Toetra
Shy	Saro-Kenatra
Sleep	Torimaso
Tail	Rambony
Wild	Dia
Yarn	Kofehy

Chemistry
Simia

Acid	Asidra
Alkaline	Alkaline
Atomic	Atomika
Carbon	Karbonina
Catalyst	Fanoitra
Chlorine	Chlore
Electron	Elektronika
Elements	Singa
Enzyme	Anzima
Hydrogen	Hydrogène
Ion	Ion
Liquid	Ranon-Javatra
Metals	Metaly
Molecule	Molekiola
Nuclear	Nokleary
Organic	Organika
Oxygen	Oksizenina
Salt	Sira
Temperature	Hafanana
Weight	Lanja

Chocolate
Sôkôla

Antioxidant	Antioxidant
Bitter	Mangidy
Cacao	Cacao
Calories	Kalset
Candy	Vatomamy
Caramel	Caramel
Coconut	Voanio
Delicious	Matsiro
Exotic	Vahiny
Favorite	Toerana Tena
Ingredient	Ilaina
Peanuts	Voanjo
Powder	Vovoka
Quality	Kalitao
Sugar	Siramamy
Sweet	Mamy
Taste	Tsiro

Circus
Fampisehoana

Acrobat	Acrobat
Animals	Biby
Balloons	Balaonina
Candy	Vatomamy
Costume	Akanjo
Elephant	Elefanta
Entertain	Voly
Juggler	Juggler
Lion	Liona
Magic	Ody
Monkey	Gidro
Music	Mozika
Parade	Matso
Show	Seho
Spectacular	Mahatalanjona
Tent	Lay
Ticket	Tapakila
Tiger	Tigra
Trick	Fitaka

Clothes
Akanjo

Apron	Aprona
Belt	Fehin-Kibo
Blouse	Blouse
Bracelet	Haitraitra
Dress	Akanjo
Fashion	Lamaody
Gloves	Fonon-Tanana
Hat	Satroka
Jacket	Palitao
Jeans	Jeans
Jewelry	Firavaka
Necklace	Rojo
Pants	Pataloha
Sandals	Kapa
Scarf	Fehy
Shirt	Lobaka
Shoe	Kiraro
Skirt	Zipo
Slippers	Kapany
Sweater	Sweater

Coffee
Kafe

Acidic	Asidra
Beverage	Zava-Pisotro
Bitter	Mangidy
Black	Mainty
Caffeine	Kafeina
Cream	Fanosotra
Cup	Kapoaka
Filter	Sivana
Flavor	Tsiro
Grind	Grind
Liquid	Ranon-Javatra
Milk	Ronono
Morning	Maraina
Origin	Fiaviana
Price	Price
Sugar	Siramamy
Water	Rano

Colors
Loko

Azure	Azure
Beige	Beige
Black	Mainty
Blue	Manga
Brown	Brown
Cyan	Cyan
Fuchsia	Fuchsia
Green	Maitso
Grey	Gray
Indigo	Indigo
Magenta	Magenta
Orange	Voasary
Pink	Mavokely
Purple	Purple
Red	Mena
Sepia	Sepia
Violet	Violet
White	Fotsy
Yellow	Mavo

Cooking Tools
Fitaovana Mahandro Sakafo

Blender	Blender
Colander	Colander
Cutlery	Cutlery
Fork	Fork
Grater	Grater
Juicer	Juicer
Kettle	Kettle
Knife	Antsy
Oven	Lafaoro
Scissors	Hety
Spatula	Spatula
Spoon	Sotro
Stove	Fatana
Strainer	Strainer
Thermometer	Mpanakoitra
Toaster	Toaster

Countries #1
Firenena #1

Brazil	Brezila
Canada	Kanada
Egypt	Ejipta
Finland	Finlande
Germany	Alemaina
Iraq	Irak
Israel	Israely
Italy	Italia
Latvia	Letonja
Libya	Libya
Morocco	Maraoka
Nicaragua	Nikaragoà
Norway	Norvezy
Panama	Panama
Poland	Polonina
Romania	Romania
Senegal	Sénégal
Spain	Espaina
Venezuela	Venezoela
Vietnam	Vietnam

Countries #2
Firenena #2

Albania	Albania
Denmark	Danemark
Ethiopia	Etiopia
Greece	Gresy
Haiti	Haiti
Jamaica	Jamaika
Japan	Japon
Laos	Laos
Lebanon	Libanona
Liberia	Liberia
Mexico	Meksika
Nepal	Nepal
Nigeria	Nizeria
Pakistan	Pakistan
Russia	Rosia
Somalia	Somalia
Sudan	Sodana
Syria	Syria
Uganda	Ouganda
Ukraine	Okraina

Dance
Mandihy

Academy	Akademia
Art	Kanto
Body	Vatana
Choreography	Koreografia
Classical	Kilasika
Culture	Kolontsaina
Emotion	Fihetseham-Po
Grace	Fahasoavana
Movement	Hetsika
Music	Mozika
Partner	Mpiara-Miasa
Posture	Fihetsika
Rehearsal	Famerenana
Rhythm	Rhythm
Visual	Maso

Days and Months
Ny Andro sy ny Volana

April	Aprily
August	Aogositra
Calendar	Kalandrie
February	Febroary
Friday	Zoma
January	Janoary
July	Jolay
March	Diabe
Monday	Alatsinainy
Month	Volana
November	Novambra
October	Oktobra
Saturday	Asabotsy
September	Septambra
Sunday	Alahady
Thursday	Alakamisy
Tuesday	Talata
Wednesday	Alarobia
Week	Herinandro
Year	Taona

Driving
Mitondra Fiara

Brakes	Freins
Bridges	Tetezana
Car	Car
Danger	Loza
Driver	Mpamily
Fuel	Fel
Garage	Garage
Insurance	Fiantohana
Map	Map
Motor	Maotera
Motorcycle	Môtô
Police	Polisy
Road	Lalana
Safety	Fiarovana
Speed	Haingo
Street	Eny An-Dalana
Transportation	Fitaterana
Truck	Kamiao
Tunnel	Tonelina

Electricity
Ny Herinaratra

Battery	Bateria
Cable	Cable
Electric	Herinaratra
Equipment	Fitaovana
Generator	Gropy
Lamp	Jiro
Laser	Laser
Magnet	Andriamby
Negative	Ratsy
Network	Rezo
Objects	Zavatra
Positive	Tsara
Quantity	Be
Socket	Socket
Storage	Fitehirizana
Telephone	Telefaonina
Television	Televizion

Energy
Angovo

Battery	Bateria
Carbon	Karbonina
Diesel	Diesel
Electric	Herinaratra
Electron	Elektronika
Engine	Injenie
Entropy	Entropy
Fuel	Fel
Gasoline	Lasantsy
Heat	Hafanana
Hydrogen	Hydrogène
Industry	Orinasa
Motor	Maotera
Nuclear	Nokleary
Photon	Photon
Pollution	Fandotoana
Renewable	Azo Havaozina
Steam	Etona
Turbine	Turbine
Wind	Rivotra

Engineering
Injenioria

Angle	Zoro
Axis	Axis
Calculation	Kajy
Construction	Fanorenana
Depth	Lalina
Diagram	Kisary
Diameter	Savaivony
Diesel	Diesel
Dimensions	Lafiny
Distribution	Fizarana
Energy	Angovo
Engine	Injenie
Gears	Gears
Levers	Levers
Liquid	Ranon-Javatra
Machine	Milina
Measurement	Fandrefesana
Motor	Maotera
Strength	Hery
Structure	Rafitra

Family
Fianakaviana

Ancestor	Razambe
Aunt	Nenitoa
Brother	Rahalahy
Child	Zaza
Childhood	Fahazazana
Children	Ankizy
Cousin	Mpiray Tam-Po
Daughter	Vavy
Father	Ray
Grandchild	Zafikely
Grandfather	Dadabe
Grandmother	Bebe
Grandson	Zafikeliny
Husband	Lehilahy
Mother	Reny
Nephew	Nephew
Paternal	Paterina
Sister	Rahavavy
Uncle	Dadatoa
Wife	Vady

Farm #1
Toeram-Pambolena #1

Agriculture	Fambolena
Bee	Betsabe
Bison	Ombidia
Calf	Ombilahy Kely
Cat	Saka
Chicken	Akoho
Cow	Ombivavy
Crow	Crow
Dog	Alika
Donkey	Anjay
Fence	Fefy
Fertilizer	Zezika
Field	Saha
Goat	Osy
Hay	Hay
Honey	Tantely
Horse	Soavaly
Rice	Vary
Seeds	Voa
Water	Rano

Farm #2
Toeram-Pambolena #2

Animals	Biby
Barley	Barley
Barn	Barn
Corn	Katsaka
Duck	Gana
Farmer	Mpamboly
Food	Sakafo
Fruit	Voankazo
Geese	Gisa
Lamb	Zanak'Ondry
Llama	Llama
Meadow	Meadow
Milk	Ronono
Orchard	Saham
Ripe	Masaka
Sheep	Ondry
Tractor	Tctor
Vegetable	Legioma
Wheat	Vary

Fashion
Lamaody

Boutique	Boutique
Buttons	Bokotra
Clothing	Fitafiana
Comfortable	Aina
Elegant	Kanto
Embroidery	Amboradara
Expensive	Lafo
Fabric	Lamba
Lace	Dantelina
Measurements	Fandrefesana
Modern	Maoderina
Modest	Tsotra
Original	Original
Style	Fomba
Texture	Mihasimba
Trend	Fironana

Fishing
Fanjonoana

Bait	Jono
Basket	Harona
Beach	Torapasika
Boat	Sambo
Cook	Cook
Equipment	Fitaovana
Exaggeration	Manitatra
Fins	Vombony
Gills	Gills
Hook	Hook
Jaw	Jaw
Lake	Farihy
Ocean	Oseana
Patience	Faharetana
River	Renirano
Season	Vanim-Potoana
Water	Rano
Weight	Lanja

Flowers
Voninkazo

Clover	Clover
Daffodil	Daffodil
Daisy	Daisy
Dandelion	Dandelion
Gardenia	Gardenia
Hibiscus	Hibiscus
Jasmine	Jasmine
Lavender	Lavender
Lilac	Lilac
Lily	Lily
Magnolia	Magnolia
Orchid	Orkid
Passionflower	Passionflower
Peony	Peony
Petal	Petal
Plumeria	Plumeria
Poppy	Poppy
Rose	Rose
Sunflower	Tanamasoandro
Tulip	Tulip

Food #1
Sakafo #1

Apricot	Apricot
Barley	Barley
Basil	Basil
Cake	Cake
Carrot	Karaoty
Cinnamon	Kanelina
Garlic	Tongolo Gasy
Milk	Ronono
Onion	Tongolo
Peanut	Voanjo
Pear	Poara
Salad	Salady
Salt	Sira
Soup	Lasopy
Spinach	Epinara
Strawberry	Frezy
Sugar	Siramamy
Tofu	Tofu
Tuna	Thon
Turnip	Turnip

Food #2
Sakafo #2

Apple	Paoma
Artichoke	Arika
Banana	Akondro
Bread	Mofo
Broccoli	Broccoli
Celery	Seleria
Cheese	Fromazy
Cherry	Serizy
Chicken	Akoho
Chocolate	Sôkôlà
Egg	Atody
Eggplant	Baranjely
Fish	Trondro
Grape	Voalop
Ham	Ham
Kiwi	Kiwi
Mushroom	Holatra
Tomato	Voatabia
Wheat	Vary
Yogurt	Yogurt

Force and Gravity
Ny Hery sy ny Hery Misin

Axis	Axis
Center	Centre
Discovery	Nahitana
Distance	Elanelana
Dynamic	Dynamic
Expansion	Fanitarana
Impact	Fiantraikany
Magnetism	Magnetism
Magnitude	Maridrefy
Mechanics	Haihetsika
Orbit	Orbit
Physics	Fizìka
Planets	Planeta
Pressure	Tsindry
Speed	Haingo
Time	Fotoana
Weight	Lanja

Fruit
Voankazo

Apple	Paoma
Apricot	Apricot
Avocado	Zavoka
Banana	Akondro
Berry	Berry
Cherry	Serizy
Coconut	Voanio
Fig	Avil
Grape	Voalop
Guava	Goavy
Kiwi	Kiwi
Mango	Manga
Melon	Voatavo
Nectarine	Nectarine
Orange	Voasary
Papaya	Papay
Peach	Paiso
Pear	Poara
Pineapple	Mananasy
Raspberry	Raspberry

Garden
Zaridaina

Bench	Bench
Bush	Bush
Fence	Fefy
Flower	Voninkazo
Garage	Garage
Garden	Zaridaina
Grass	Ahitra
Hose	Hose
Lawn	Bozaka
Orchard	Saham
Pond	Dobo
Rake	Karohy
Rocks	Vato
Soil	Tany
Terrace	Tanimbariza
Trampoline	Trampoline
Tree	Hazo
Weeds	Ahidratsy

Geography
Jeografia

Altitude	Altitude
Atlas	Atlas
City	Tanàna
Continent	Kaontinanta
Country	Firenena
Elevation	Isam-Ponina
Equator	Ekoatera
Hemisphere	Bolantany
Island	Nosy
Latitude	Latitude
Map	Map
Meridian	Meridian
North	Avaratra
Ocean	Oseana
Region	Faritra
River	Renirano
Sea	Ranomasina
South	Atsimo
Territory	Faritany
West	Andrefana

Geology
Haibolantany

Acid	Asidra
Calcium	Kalsioma
Cavern	Zohy
Continent	Kaontinanta
Coral	Coral
Crystals	Kristaly
Cycles	Tsingerina
Earthquake	Horohorontany
Erosion	Riaka
Fossil	Fôsily
Geyser	Geyser
Lava	Lava
Layer	Sosona
Minerals	Mineraly
Plateau	Plateau
Quartz	Quartz
Salt	Sira
Stalactite	Stalactite
Stone	Vato
Volcano	Volkano

Geometry
Rafitsary

Angle	Zoro
Calculation	Kajy
Circle	Faribolana
Curve	Curve
Diameter	Savaivony
Dimension	Lafiny
Equation	Mira
Height	Hahavony
Horizontal	Marindrano
Logic	Logic
Mass	Lamesa
Median	Median
Number	Isa
Parallel	Mitovy
Proportion	Arakaraka
Segment	Ampahany
Surface	Faritra
Symmetry	Symmetry
Theory	Teoria
Triangle	Telozoro

Government
Fitondram-Panjakana

Citizenship	Zom-Pirenena
Civil	Sivily
Democracy	Demokrasia
District	Distrika
Equality	Fitoviana
Judicial	Fitsarana
Justice	Rariny
Law	Lalàna
Leader	Mpitarika
Liberty	Fahafahana
Monument	Tsangambato
Nation	Firenena
Politics	Politika
Rights	Zo
Speech	Kabary
State	Fanjakana
Symbol	Mariky

Gymnastics
Fanatanjahan-Tena

Agility	Fahaizana
Chalk	Tsaoka
Coach	Mpanazatra
Combinations	Tsikombakomba
Gymnasium	Kianja
Gymnasts	Gymnasts
Hands	Tanana
Hoop	Hoop
Individual	Olona
Judge	Mpitsara
Jumping	Mitsambikina
Leotards	Leotards
Music	Mozika
Routine	Fahazarana
Strength	Hery
Team	Ekipa

Hair Types
Karazana Volo

Bald	Sola
Black	Mainty
Blond	Blond
Braided	Mirandrana
Brown	Brown
Curls	Curl
Curly	Olioly
Dry	Maina
Gray	Grey
Healthy	Salama
Long	Ela
Shiny	Mamirapiratra
Short	Fohy
Silver	Volafotsy
Soft	Malefaka
Thick	Matevina
Thin	Manify
Wavy	Wavy
White	Fotsy

Health and Wellness #1
Fahasalamana sy Fahasala

Active	Miasa
Bacteria	Bakteria
Bones	Taolana
Doctor	Dokotera
Fracture	Tapaka
Habit	Fahazarana
Height	Hahavony
Hormones	Hormonina
Hunger	Hanoanana
Injury	Ratra
Medicine	Fanafody
Muscles	Hozatra
Pharmacy	Levitra
Posture	Fihetsika
Relaxation	Fialam-Boly
Skin	Hoditra
Treatment	Fitsaboana
Virus	Virosy

Health and Wellness #2
Fahasalamana sy Fahasala

Allergy	Alerjia
Anatomy	Anatomy
Appetite	Komana
Blood	Ra
Calorie	Kalorie
Diet	Sakafo
Digestion	Digestion
Disease	Aretina
Energy	Angovo
Genetics	Fototarazo
Healthy	Salama
Hospital	Hopitaly
Hygiene	Fahadiovana
Massage	Fanorana
Mood	Toe-Po
Recovery	Sitrana
Sleep	Torimaso
Stress	Adin - Tsaina
Vitamin	Vitaminina
Weight	Lanja

Herbalism
Herbalism

Aromatic	Manitra
Basil	Basil
Beneficial	Mahasoa
Culinary	Culinary
Fennel	Fennel
Flavor	Tsiro
Flower	Voninkazo
Garden	Zaridaina
Garlic	Tongolo Gasy
Green	Maitso
Ingredient	Ilaina
Lavender	Lavender
Marjoram	Marjoram
Mint	Mint
Oregano	Oregano
Parsley	Persily
Plant	Zavamaniry
Rosemary	Rosemary
Saffron	Safrona
Tarragon	Tarragon

Hiking
Tongotra Lavitra

Animals	Biby
Boots	Kiraro
Cliff	Harambato
Climate	Toetrandro
Hazards	Loza
Heavy	Mavesatra
Map	Map
Mosquitoes	Moka
Nature	Toetra
Parks	Zaridaina
Preparation	Fiomanana
Stones	Vato
Summit	Vovonana
Sun	Masoandro
Tired	Reraka
Water	Rano
Wild	Dia

House
Trano

Basement	Ambany Rihana
Broom	Kifafa
Curtains	Lay
Door	Varavarana
Fence	Fefy
Fireplace	Am-Patana
Floor	Tany
Furniture	Fanaka
Garage	Garage
Garden	Zaridaina
Keys	Fanalahidy
Kitchen	Lakozia
Lamp	Jiro
Library	Tahtery
Mirror	Fitaratra
Roof	Tafo
Room	Efitrano
Shower	Fandroana
Wall	Rindrina
Window	Fikandrana

Human Body
Vatan'ny Olombelona

Ankle	Ankle
Blood	Ra
Bones	Taolana
Brain	Atidoha
Chin	Chin
Ear	Sofina
Elbow	Kiho
Face	Tena
Finger	Rantsan-
Hand	Tanana
Head	Loha
Heart	Fo
Jaw	Jaw
Knee	Lohalika
Leg	Tongotra
Mouth	Vava
Neck	Tenda
Nose	Orona
Shoulder	Sorony
Skin	Hoditra

Insects
Bibikely

Ant	Tafio - Doko
Aphid	Aphid
Bee	Betsabe
Beetle	Voangory
Butterfly	Lolo
Cicada	Cicada
Cockroach	Kalalao
Dragonfly	Angidina
Flea	Parasy
Grasshopper	Valala
Hornet	Hornet
Ladybug	Ladybug
Larva	Larva
Mantis	Mantis
Mosquito	Moka
Termite	Termite
Wasp	Wasp
Worm	Kankana

Jazz
Jazz

Album	Rakikira
Applause	Tehaka
Artist	Mpanakanto
Composer	Mpamoron-Kira
Concert	Fampisehoana
Drums	Amponga
Emphasis	Fanamafisana
Famous	Malaza
Favorites	Favoris
Genre	Genre
Improvisation	Fanambarana
Music	Mozika
New	Vaovao
Old	Taloha
Orchestra	Orkesitra
Rhythm	Rhythm
Song	Hira
Style	Fomba
Talent	Talenta
Technique	Teknika

Landscapes
Ny Endriky

Beach	Torapasika
Cave	Lava-Bato
Cliff	Harambato
Desert	Efitra
Geyser	Geyser
Glacier	Glacier
Hill	Havoana
Iceberg	Iceberg
Island	Nosy
Lake	Farihy
Oasis	Oasis
Ocean	Oseana
Peninsula	Saikinosy
River	Renirano
Sea	Ranomasina
Swamp	Honahona
Tundra	Tundra
Valley	Lohasaha
Volcano	Volkano
Waterfall	Riandrano

Literature
Ny Literatiora

Analogy	Analogy
Analysis	Fanadihadiana
Author	Mpanoratra
Comparison	Fampitahana
Conclusion	Famaranana
Critique	Fanakianana
Description	Description
Dialogue	Takila
Fiction	Nofohezina
Genre	Genre
Metaphor	Metafira
Narrator	Mpitantara
Novel	Tantara
Poem	Tononkalo
Rhyme	Rhyme
Rhythm	Rhythm
Style	Fomba
Theme	Foto-Kevitra
Tragedy	Loza

Mammals
Ny Biby Mampinono

Bear	Bera
Beaver	Beaver
Bull	Omby
Cat	Saka
Coyote	Coyote
Dog	Alika
Dolphin	Feso
Elephant	Elefanta
Fox	Fox
Giraffe	Zirafy
Gorilla	Rajako
Horse	Soavaly
Kangaroo	Kangaroo
Lion	Liona
Monkey	Gidro
Rabbit	Bitro
Sheep	Ondry
Whale	Trozona
Wolf	Wolf
Zebra	Zebra

Math
Matematika

Arithmetic	Rafitrisa
Circumference	Circumference
Decimal	Decimal
Diameter	Savaivony
Equation	Mira
Exponent	Exponent
Fraction	Ampahany
Geometry	Rafitsary
Numbers	Isa
Parallel	Mitovy
Parallelogram	Parallelogram
Perimeter	Paritra
Perpendicular	Perpendicular
Polygon	Marolafy
Rectangle	Mahitsi-
Sum	Vola
Symmetry	Symmetry
Triangle	Telozoro
Volume	Boky

Measurements
Fandrefesana

Byte	Byte
Centimeter	Centimeter
Decimal	Decimal
Depth	Lalina
Gram	Gram
Height	Hahavony
Inch	Mirefy
Kilogram	Kilao
Kilometer	Kilometatra
Length	Halavany
Liter	Litatra
Mass	Lamesa
Minute	Minitra
Ounce	Grama
Pint	Pint
Ton	Taonina
Volume	Boky
Weight	Lanja

Meditation
Ny Fisaintsainana

Acceptance	Ny Fanekena
Awake	Mifohaza
Breathing	Miaina
Calm	Tony
Clarity	Mazava
Compassion	Fangorahana
Emotions	Fihetseham-Po
Habits	Fahazarana
Happiness	Fahasambarana
Mental	Ara-Tsaina
Mind	Saina
Movement	Hetsika
Music	Mozika
Nature	Toetra
Observation	Fandinihana
Peace	Fiadanana
Perspective	Fomba Fijery
Posture	Fihetsika
Silence	Fahanginana
Thoughts	Eritreritra

Music
Mozika

Album	Rakikira
Ballad	Ballad
Chorus	Chorus
Classical	Kilasika
Eclectic	Ekilekitika
Harmony	Firindrana
Instrument	Fitaovana
Lyrical	Tonon
Melody	Fiderana
Microphone	Mikrô
Musician	Mozika
Opera	Opéra
Poetic	Tononkalo
Rhythm	Rhythm
Rhythmic	Ngadona
Sing	Hira
Singer	Mpihira
Tempo	Tempo
Vocal	Feo

Musical Instruments
Zava-Maneno

Banjo	Banjo
Bassoon	Bassoon
Cello	Lokangabe
Chimes	Chimes
Drum	Amponga
Flute	Sodina
Gong	Gong
Guitar	Gitara
Harmonica	Harmonica
Harp	Harp
Mandolin	Mandolin
Marimba	Marimba
Oboe	Oboe
Percussion	Percussion
Piano	Piano
Saxophone	Saxophone
Tambourine	Tambourine
Trombone	Trombone
Trumpet	Trompetra
Violin	Lokanga

Mythology
Angano

Archetype	Archetype
Behavior	Fitondrantena
Beliefs	Finoana
Creation	Famoronana
Creature	Zavaboary
Culture	Kolontsaina
Deities	Andriamanitra
Disaster	Loza
Heaven	Lanitra
Hero	Maherifo
Jealousy	Fialonana
Labyrinth	Labyrinta
Legend	Angano
Lightning	Tselatra
Revenge	Valifaly
Strength	Hery
Thunder	Varatra
Warrior	Mpiady

Nature
Ny Natiora

Animals	Biby
Arctic	Actic
Beauty	Hatsaratarehy
Bees	Tantely
Clouds	Rahona
Desert	Efitra
Dynamic	Dynamic
Erosion	Riaka
Fog	Zavona
Foliage	Ravina
Forest	Ala
Glacier	Glacier
River	Renirano
Serene	Tony
Shelter	Fialofana
Tropical	Tany Mafana
Vital	Zava-Dehibe
Wild	Dia

Nutrition
Ny Sakafo

Appetite	Komana
Bitter	Mangidy
Calories	Kalset
Carbohydrates	Gliosida
Diet	Sakafo
Digestion	Digestion
Edible	Fihinana
Fermentation	Fermentation
Flavor	Tsiro
Habits	Fahazarana
Health	Fahasalamana
Healthy	Salama
Liquids	Ranon-Javatra
Proteins	Proteinina
Quality	Kalitao
Sauce	Saosy
Spices	Zava-Manitra
Toxin	Poxin
Vitamin	Vitaminina
Weight	Lanja

Ocean
Ranomasimbe

Boat	Sambo
Coral	Coral
Crab	Foza
Dolphin	Feso
Eel	Eel
Fish	Trondro
Jellyfish	Jellyfish
Octopus	Horita
Oyster	Oyster
Salt	Sira
Seaweed	Ahidrano
Shark	Antsantsa
Shrimp	Shrimp
Sponge	Sponge
Storm	Drivotra
Tides	Samonta
Tuna	Thon
Turtle	Sokatra
Waves	Onja
Whale	Trozona

Photography
Sary

Black	Mainty
Camera	Fakantsary
Color	Loko
Contrast	Mifanohitra
Darkness	Haizina
Definition	Famaritana
Exhibition	Fampirantiana
Format	Endrika
Frame	Frame
Lighting	Jiro
Object	Zavatra
Perspective	Fomba Fijery
Portrait	Portrait
Shadows	Aloka
Texture	Mihasimba
Visual	Maso

Physics
Ny Fizika

Acceleration	Haingana
Atom	Tsivaky
Chaos	Korontana
Chemical	Simika
Density	Hakitroky
Electron	Elektronika
Engine	Injenie
Expansion	Fanitarana
Experiment	Fanandramana
Formula	Formula
Frequency	Hatetika
Magnetism	Magnetism
Mass	Lamesa
Mechanics	Haihetsika
Molecule	Molekiola
Nuclear	Nokleary
Particle	Sombiny
Relativity	Relativits
Speed	Haingo
Velocity	Veloma

Plants
Ny Zava-Maniry

Bamboo	Bambo
Bean	Bean
Berry	Berry
Botany	Botany
Bush	Bush
Cactus	Raozy
Fertilizer	Zezika
Flora	Flora
Flower	Voninkazo
Foliage	Ravina
Forest	Ala
Garden	Zaridaina
Grass	Ahitra
Ivy	Ivy
Moss	Moss
Petal	Petal
Root	Faka
Stem	Sampa
Tree	Hazo
Vegetation	Zavamaniry

Professions #1
Fiekem #1

Ambassador	Masoivoho
Artist	Mpanakanto
Astronomer	Astronoma
Attorney	Mpisolovava
Cartographer	Cartographer
Coach	Mpanazatra
Dancer	Mpandihy
Doctor	Dokotera
Editor	Mpanadihtor
Firefighter	Mpamono Afo
Hunter	Hunter
Jeweler	Firavaka
Mechanic	Mpanamboatra
Musician	Mozika
Pharmacist	Pharmacist
Plumber	Plumber
Psychologist	Psikology
Sailor	Tantsambo
Scientist	Mpahay Siansa
Tailor	Tailor

Professions #2
Fiekem #2

Astronaut	Mpanamory
Biologist	Mpikaroka
Chemist	Mpahay Simia
Dentist	Mpitsabo Nify
Detective	Mpitsongodia
Engineer	Injeniera
Farmer	Mpamboly
Gardener	Zaridaina
Illustrator	Sary
Journalist	Mpanao Gazety
Librarian	Tranomboky
Linguist	Momba ny Teny
Painter	Mpanasoa
Philosopher	Filozofa
Photographer	Mpaka Sary
Physician	Dokotera
Professor	Profesora
Surgeon	Mpandidy
Teacher	Mpampianatra
Zoologist	Zoologist

Psychology
Psikolojia

Appointment	Fanendrena
Assessment	Fanombanana
Behavior	Fitondrantena
Childhood	Fahazazana
Clinical	Pitsaboana
Cognition	Cognition
Conflict	Fifandirana
Dreams	Nofy
Ideas	Hevitra
Influences	Fitaoman
Perception	Fomba Fijery
Personality	Toetra
Problem	Olana
Reality	Zava-Misy
Sensation	Fihetseham-Po
Subconscious	Nohaniny
Therapy	Fitsaboana
Thoughts	Eritreritra

Restaurant #1
Trano Fisakafoanana #1

Allergy	Alerjia
Bread	Mofo
Cashier	Cashier
Chicken	Akoho
Coffee	Kafe
Food	Sakafo
Ingredients	Fangaro
Kitchen	Lakozia
Knife	Antsy
Meat	Hena
Menu	Tolotra
Napkin	Napkin
Reservation	Famandrihana
Sauce	Saosy
Spicy	Masiaka
Waitress	Waitress

Restaurant #2
Trano Fisakafoanana #2

Appetizer	Appetizer
Beverage	Zava-Pisotro
Cake	Cake
Chair	Seza
Delicious	Matsiro
Dinner	Sakafo Hariva
Eggs	Atody
Fish	Trondro
Fork	Fork
Fruit	Voankazo
Ice	Ranomandry
Noodles	Paty
Salad	Salady
Salt	Sira
Soup	Lasopy
Spices	Zava-Manitra
Spoon	Sotro
Vegetables	Legioma
Waiter	Servera
Water	Rano

Science
Ny Siansa

Atom	Tsivaky
Chemical	Simika
Climate	Toetrandro
Evolution	Evolisiona
Experiment	Fanandramana
Fact	Zava-Misy
Fossil	Fôsily
Hypothesis	Petra-Kevitra
Laboratory	Laboratoara
Method	Fomba
Minerals	Mineraly
Molecules	Molekiola
Nature	Toetra
Observation	Fandinihana
Particles	Poti
Physics	Fizìka
Plants	Zavamaniry
Scientist	Mpahay Siansa

Science Fiction
Ny Siansa ny Tantara For

Atomic	Atomika
Books	Boky
Cinema	Sarimaho
Clones	Clones
Distant	Lavitra
Dystopia	Dystopia
Explosion	Fipoahana
Extreme	Tafahoatra
Fantastic	Mahafinaritra
Fire	Afo
Futuristic	Futuristic
Galaxy	Galaxy
Illusion	Nofinofy
Mysterious	Mistery
Novels	Tantara
Oracle	Oracle
Planet	Planeta
Realistic	Zava-Misy
Technology	Teknolojia
Utopia	Utopia

Scientific Disciplines
Ara-Tsiansa ny Fitsipika

Anatomy	Anatomy
Archaeology	Arkeolojia
Astronomy	Astronoma
Biochemistry	Biochemistry
Biology	Haiaina
Botany	Botany
Chemistry	Simia
Ecology	Ecology
Geology	Tany
Immunology	Fitandremam
Kinesiology	Kinesiology
Linguistics	Tenuistics
Mechanics	Haihetsika
Meteorology	Toetrandro
Mineralogy	Mineralogy
Neurology	Neurology
Physiology	Fisiolojia
Psychology	Psychology
Sociology	Sosiolojia
Zoology	Haibiby

Shapes
Manamboatra

Arc	Arc
Circle	Faribolana
Cone	Cone
Corner	Corner
Cube	Goba
Curve	Curve
Cylinder	Varingarin'I
Edges	Sisiny
Ellipse	Ellipse
Hyperbola	Hyperbola
Line	Andalana
Polygon	Marolafy
Prism	Prism
Pyramid	Piramida
Rectangle	Mahitsi-
Side	Side
Triangle	Telozoro

Spices
Zava-Manitra

Bitter	Mangidy
Cardamom	Cardamom
Cinnamon	Kanelina
Clove	Clove
Coriander	Drafy
Cumin	Komina
Curry	Curry
Fennel	Fennel
Fenugreek	Fenugreek
Flavor	Tsiro
Garlic	Tongolo Gasy
Ginger	Sakamalaho
Licorice	Licorice
Nutmeg	Nutmeg
Onion	Tongolo
Paprika	Paprika
Saffron	Safrona
Salt	Sira
Sweet	Mamy
Vanilla	Lavanila

Technology
Ny Teknolojia

Blog	Blog
Browser	Mpitety
Bytes	Bytes
Camera	Fakantsary
Computer	Solosaina
Cursor	Kitondro
Digital	Nomerika
File	Rakitra
Internet	Internet
Message	Hafatra
Research	Fikarohana
Screen	Lamba
Security	Aro
Software	Software
Statistics	Antontan'Isa
Virtual	Virtoaly
Virus	Virosy

The Media
Ny Haino Aman-Jery

Advertisements	Dokam-Barotra
Commercial	Ara-Barotra
Communication	Fifandraisana
Digital	Nomerika
Edition	Fanontana
Education	Fanabeazana
Individual	Olona
Industry	Orinasa
Intellectual	Ara-Tsaina
Local	Local
Network	Rezo
Newspapers	Gazety
Online	Online
Photos	Sary
Public	Bahoaka
Radio	Radio
Television	Televizion

Time
Fotoana

After	Taorian'Ny
Annual	Isan-Taona
Before	Taloha
Calendar	Kalandrie
Century	Taonjato Maro
Day	Andro
Decade	Folo Taona
Future	Hoavy
Hour	Ora
Minute	Minitra
Moment	Fotoana
Month	Volana
Morning	Maraina
Night	Alina
Now	Ankehitriny
Soon	Tsy ho Ela
Today	Anio
Week	Herinandro
Year	Taona
Yesterday	Omaly

To Fill
Mba Hamenoana

Bag	Kitapo
Barrel	Barika
Basin	Basin
Basket	Harona
Bottle	Tavoahangy
Box	Efajoro
Bucket	Siny
Carton	Carton
Crate	Crate
Drawer	Vatasarihana
Envelope	Valopy
Folder	Lahatahiry
Packet	Fonosana
Pocket	Paosy
Suitcase	Suitcase
Tray	Lovia
Tube	Fantsona
Vase	Vazy

Tools
Fitaovana

Axe	Ax
Cable	Cable
Glue	Lakaoly
Hammer	Tantanana
Knife	Antsy
Ladder	Tohatra
Mallet	Mallet
Pliers	Pliers
Razor	Hareza
Rope	Tady
Ruler	Mpitondra
Scissors	Hety
Screw	Visy
Stapler	Stapler
Torch	Fanilo
Wheel	Kodiarana

Town
An-Tanàna

Bakery	Fanaova-Mofo
Bank	Bank
Cafe	Cafe
Cinema	Sarimaho
Florist	Florist
Gallery	Gallery
Hotel	Hotely
Library	Tahtery
Market	Tsena
Museum	Moseum
Pharmacy	Levitra
Salon	Salon
School	Sekoly
Stadium	Kianja
Store	Fivarotana
Supermarket	Toetoetra
Theater	Teatra
University	Oniversite
Zoo	Zoo

Universe
Izao Rehetra Izao

Asteroid	Asteroid
Astronomer	Astronoma
Atmosphere	Atmosféra
Celestial	Selestialy
Cosmic	Cosmic
Darkness	Haizina
Eon	Eon
Equator	Ekoatera
Galaxy	Galaxy
Hemisphere	Bolantany
Horizon	Horizon
Latitude	Latitude
Moon	Volana
Orbit	Orbit
Sky	Lanitra
Solar	Solar
Solstice	Solstice
Telescope	Ary
Visible	Hita Maso
Zodiac	Zodiaka

Vegetables
Legioma

Artichoke	Arika
Broccoli	Broccoli
Carrot	Karaoty
Cauliflower	Soflera
Celery	Seleria
Cucumber	Kôkômbra
Eggplant	Baranjely
Garlic	Tongolo Gasy
Ginger	Sakamalaho
Mushroom	Holatra
Olive	Olive
Onion	Tongolo
Parsley	Persily
Pea	Pea
Pumpkin	Voatavo
Radish	Radish
Salad	Salady
Spinach	Epinara
Tomato	Voatabia
Turnip	Turnip

Vehicles
Fiara

Airplane	Fiaramanidina
Bicycle	Bisikileta
Boat	Sambo
Car	Car
Caravan	Caravan
Engine	Injenie
Ferry	Baka
Helicopter	Angidimby
Motor	Maotera
Raft	Raft
Rocket	Balafomanga
Scooter	Scooter
Shuttle	Mivezivezy
Subway	Metro
Taxi	Taxi
Tires	Kodiarana
Tractor	Tctor
Truck	Kamiao
Van	Van

Visual Arts
Zavakanto Hita Maso

Architecture	Ny Maritrano
Artist	Mpanakanto
Ceramics	Seramika
Chalk	Tsaoka
Charcoal	Arina
Clay	Tanimanga
Composition	Fifehezan
Creativity	Famoronana
Easel	Easel
Film	Horonan-Tsary
Masterpiece	Sanganasa
Painting	Loko
Pen	Penina
Pencil	Pensilihazo
Perspective	Fomba Fijery
Photograph	Sary
Portrait	Portrait
Sculpture	Sary Sokitra
Stencil	Stencil
Wax	Savoka

Water
Rano

Canal	Lalana
Damp	Mando
Drinkable	Misotro
Evaporation	Lasa Etona
Flood	Safodrano
Frost	Fanala
Geyser	Geyser
Humidity	Hatondra
Hurricane	Rivo-Doza
Ice	Ranomandry
Lake	Farihy
Moisture	Hamandoana
Monsoon	Orana
Ocean	Ocean
Rain	Ny Orana
River	Renirano
Shower	Fandroana
Snow	Oram-Panala
Steam	Etona
Waves	Onja

Weather
Ny Andro

Atmosphere	Rivo-Piainana
Breeze	Tsio-Drivotra
Climate	Toetrandro
Cloud	Rahona
Drought	Hain-Tany
Dry	Maina
Fog	Zavona
Hurricane	Rivo-Doza
Ice	Ranomandry
Lightning	Helatra
Monsoon	Orana
Polar	Polar
Rainbow	Avana
Sky	Lanitra
Storm	Drivotra
Temperature	Hafanana
Thunder	Varatra
Tornado	Tornado
Tropical	Tany Mafana
Wind	Rivotra

Congratulations

You made it!

We hope you enjoyed this book as much as we enjoyed making it. We do our best to make high quality games.
These puzzles are designed in a clever way for you to learn actively while having fun!

Did you love them?

A Simple Request

Our books exist thanks your reviews. Could you help us by leaving one now?

Here is a short link which will take you to your order review page:

BestBooksActivity.com/Review50

MONSTER CHALLENGE!

Challenge #1

Ready for Your Bonus Game? We use them all the time but they are not so easy to find. Here are **Synonyms**!

Note 5 words you discovered in each of the Puzzles noted below (#21, #36, #76) and try to find 2 synonyms for each word.

Note 5 Words from *Puzzle 21*

Words	Synonym 1	Synonym 2

Note 5 Words from *Puzzle 36*

Words	Synonym 1	Synonym 2

Note 5 Words from *Puzzle 76*

Words	Synonym 1	Synonym 2

Challenge #2

Now that you are warmed-up, note 5 words you discovered in each Puzzle noted below (#9, #17, #25) and try to find 2 antonyms for each word. How many lines can you do in 20 minutes?

Note 5 Words from **Puzzle 9**

Words	Antonym 1	Antonym 2

Note 5 Words from **Puzzle 17**

Words	Antonym 1	Antonym 2

Note 5 Words from **Puzzle 25**

Words	Antonym 1	Antonym 2

Challenge #3

Wonderful, this monster challenge is nothing to you!

Ready for the last one? Choose your 10 favorite words discovered in any of the Puzzles and note them below.

1.	6.
2.	7.
3.	8.
4.	9.
5.	10.

Now, using these words and within a maximum of six sentences, your challenge is to compose a text about a person, animal or place that you love!

Tip: You can use the last blank page of this book as a draft!

Your Writing:

Explore a Unique Store
Set Up **FOR YOU!**

MEGA DEALS

BestActivityBooks.com/**TheStore**

Designed for Entertainment!

Light Up Your Brain With Unique **Gift Ideas**.

Access **Surprising** And **Essential Supplies!**

CHECK OUT OUR MONTHLY SELECTION NOW!

- Expertly Crafted Products -

NOTEBOOK:

SEE YOU SOON!

Linguas Classics Team

ENJOY FREE GAMES

NOW ON

BESTACTIVITYBOOKS.COM/FREEGAMES